TRUCKING BUSINESS STARTUP

2 Books In 1:

Step By Step Guide To Become a Successful Freight Broker

BY
JOHN LONG

STARTUP BUSINESS

© Copyright 2021 by JOHN LONG
All rights reserved.

This document is geared towards providing exact and reliable information in regards to the topic and issue covered. The publication is sold with the idea that the publisher is not required to render accounting, officially permitted, or otherwise, qualified services. If advice is necessary, legal or professional, a practiced individual in the profession should be ordered.

- From a Declaration of Principles, which was accepted and approved equally by a Committee of the American Bar Association and a Committee of Publishers and Associations.

In no way is it legal to reproduce, duplicate, or transmit any part of this document in either electronic means or printed format. Recording of this publication is strictly prohibited, and any storage of this document is not allowed unless with written permission from the publisher. All rights reserved.

The information provided herein is stated to be truthful and consistent, in that any liability, in terms of inattention or otherwise, by any usage or abuse of any policies, processes, or directions contained within is the solitary and utter responsibility of the recipient reader.

Under no circumstances will any legal responsibility or blame be held against the publisher for reparation, damages, or monetary loss due to the information herein, either directly or indirectly.

Respective authors own all copyrights not held by the publisher.

The information herein is offered for informational purposes solely and is universal as such. The presentation of the information is without a contract or any guarantee assurance.

The trademarks used are without any consent, and the publication of the trademark is without permission or backing by the trademark owner. All trademarks and brands within this book are for clarifying purposes only and are owned by the owners themselves, not affiliated with this document.

Table Of Contents

BOOK 1: OPERATOR TRUCKING BUSINESS START-UP............ 9

INTRODUCTION 11

CHAPTER 1: HISTORY OF TRUCKS AND TRUCKING BUSINESS 17
- 1.1 THE FIRST TOW TRUCK 19
- 1.2 FORKLIFT TRUCKS 20
- 1.3 MACK TRUCKS 20
- 1.4 SEMI-TRUCKS 20
- 1.5 THE EMERGENCE OF MODERN TRUCKING 21

CHAPTER 2: WHAT IS A TRUCKING BUSINESS? 23
- 2.1 WHY DO WE NEED THE TRUCKING INDUSTRY? 24
- 2.2 EMPLOYMENT 25
- 2.3 ESSENTIAL DETAILS 25
- 2.4 BASICS OF TRUCKING BUSINESS 26
- 2.5 IMPORTANT CONSIDERATIONS 26
- 2.6 DIFFERENCE BETWEEN AN OWNER-OPERATOR AND COMPANY DRIVER .. 29
- 2.7 WHY YOU SHOULD START A TRUCKING COMPANY BUSINESS 29
- 2.8 REGULATION COSTS 36

CHAPTER 3: GETTING STARTED 39
- 3.1 WHAT TO KNOW BEFORE YOU START 39
- 3.2 GETTING STARTED-GUIDE TO HOW TO START A TRUCKING BUSINESS 45
- 3.3 A COMPLETE GUIDE TO STARTING A NEW TRUCKING COMPANY 46
- 3.4 OBTAIN A TRUCKING BUSINESS LICENSE 48
- 3.5 PERMITS AND LICENSES FOR OPERATING A TRUCKING COMPANY 49
- 3.6 GET A COMMERCIAL DRIVER'S LICENSE 50
- 3.7 BUSINESS STRUCTURE AND DOCUMENTATION 59
- 3.8 START-UP COSTS FOR AN OWNER-OPERATOR 62
- 3.9 BUYING VEHICLES: NEW VS. USED 75
- 3.10 BUYING A SEMI-TRUCK AS AN OWNER-OPERATOR 76
- 3.11 LEASING A SEMI-TRUCK AS AN OWNER-OPERATOR 77
- 3.12 LEASE TYPES 78
- 3.13 DIFFERENCE BETWEEN AN OWNER OPERATOR TRUCK DRIVER AND A COMPANY TRUCK DRIVER 94
- 3.14 BENEFITS OF OWNER OPERATOR TRUCKING BUSINESS...... 95

CHAPTER 4: TRUCKING BUSINESS TYPES 101
- 4.1 FULL TRUCKLOAD CARRIERS 102
- 4.2 PRIVATE FLEETS 103

4.3 Less-than-truckload carriers 104
4.4 Couriers 106
4.5 Backhaul 106
4.6 Household Movers 108
4.7 Inter-modal 108
4.8 Flatbed trucking service 109
4.9 Refrigerated trucks or reefer trucks 110
4.10 Expedited trucking service 111
4.11 White glove service 111
4.12 Door-to-Door 111
4.13 Business to Business 112
4.14 Heavy Haul or Specialized 113
4.15 Tanker 113
4.16 Bull Hauler 114
4.17 Auto Hauler 114
4.18 Container Hauler 114
4.19 Hopper (or Grain Hauler) 114

CHAPTER 5: MARKETING STRATEGY FOR OWNER OPERATOR TRUCKING BUSINESS 115

5.1 Learn to distinguish yourself from the competition 116
5.2 Manage the transportation costs effectively 119
5.3 Be reliable if you want to grow 119
5.4 Use smart tactics 119
5.5 Optimize the processes 120
5.6 Control overheads 121
5.7 Avoid mistakes 121
5.8 Create an organizational structure 122
5.9 Work on value addition 122
5.10 Know about the customer's business 122
5.11 Establish business relationships 123
5.12 Work for efficient data management 123
5.13 Make a customer mix 124
5.14 Be part of a Network 124
5.15 Be proactive 124
5.16 Develop reputation 125
5.17 Learn to control cost 125
5.18 Prepare for the future 126
5.19 Don't waste time inventing new ideas 126
5.20 Get rid of old trucks 127
5.21 Maintain a broad and diverse customer base 127
5.22 Get in the spotlight 127
5.23 Be open to evolution 128

5.24 Get industry experience as well as research 128
5.25 Protect your reputation 128
5.26 Set prices 129
5.27 Use advertising and marketing techniques that work 129
5.28 Set your goals and objectives 130
5.29 Positioning and growth 132
5.30 SWOT analysis 132
5.31 Pricing Strategy 136
5.32 Geographical Pricing 140
5.33 Top and effective ways to market your trucking business 141
5.34 Partner with Trade Publications 143
5.35 How to establish a business niche and brand image? 147

CHAPTER 6: MANAGING HUMAN RESOURCE AND BUILDING FLEET FOR TRUCKING BUSINESS 163

6.1 Managing your business finances and raising the desired start-up capital 164
6.2 Choose a suitable location for your business 168
6.3 Expense Management 169
6.4 Choose your market niche wisely 175
6.5 Know when to outsource and insource business functions 176
6.6 Final thoughts 177
6.7 Plan ahead 178
6.8 Develop a loyal customer base 182
6.9 Remember it is a business 182
6.10 Hiring drivers and other employees 183
6.11 How to find your customers? 184
6.12 How to sell your service? 185
6.13 Create a customer lead list 185
6.14 Start with a customer email or phone call 186
6.15 How to scale your business? 191
6.16 Master your business finances 193
6.17 Commitment to providing the best service 194
6.18 Define plans for business growth 194
6.19 Look for clients with load boards and freight brokers 195
6.20 Be smart 195
6.21 Manage your cash flow wisely 195

CHAPTER 7: THE MOST COMMON REASONS WHY TRUCKING BUSINESS FAILS 198

7.1 Poor management 199
7.2 Bad managers make bad business decisions 200
7.3 Poor management of finances 201
7.4 No clue of how much to charge for your services 202

7.5 Violating rules and not minding compliance 203
7.6 Not getting help when you need it 203
7.7 Problems with the economy or the industry 204
7.8 Driver Shortage 205
7.9 Not meeting customer expectations correctly 205
7.10 Not investing in technology 206
7.11 Choosing the wrong people as partners 208
7.12 Not knowing the real cost per mile 208

CHAPTER 8: THE PROS AND CONS OF A TRUCKING BUSINESS 210

8.1 Pros of trucking business 210
8.2 Cons of the trucking business 212
8.3 Secrets and tips to increase profit and have a successful trucking business 214

BOOK 2: FREIGHT BROKER 222

INTRODUCTION 224

CHAPTER 1: RESPONSIBILITIES OF FREIGHT BROKER 226

CHAPTER 2: LICENSING AND BUSINESS REGISTRATION 230

2.1 Establish a Business Structure 231
2.2 Submit an OP-1 Form 232
2.3 Get a Surety Bond (BMC-84) 233
2.4 Select a Process Agent 235
2.5 Register the Brokerage 235
2.6 What to Do After Getting a License 236

CHAPTER 3: HOW IMPORTANT IS KNOWING YOUR TARGET MARKET 238

3.1 Knowing your target market is important, but you also need buyer personas in today's digital world. 239
3.2 Inbound marketing success also requires adaptability. 240

CHAPTER 4: EFFECTIVE BUSINESS PLAN 242

4.1 Outline of a Freight Trucking Business Plan 243

CHAPTER 5: MARKETING AND FINDING CLIENTS 246

5.1 Marketing 247
5.2 Finding clients 250

CHAPTER 6: HOW TO BECOME A SUCCESSFUL FREIGHT BROKER AND GROW YOUR BUSINESS 256

6.1 Acquire industry experience 257
6.2 Recognize the Business Costs 257
6.3 Meet with the Licensing Requirements 258
6.4 Understanding the Differences Between a Trust and a bond 259
6.5 Build the Business Relationships 259
6.6 Have a Communication System 260
6.7 Marketing the Business 260
6.8 Put in Effort and Time 261
6.9 Gain an understanding of the market 261
6.10 Invest into your differentials 262

CHAPTER 7: HOW TO FIND CARRIERS AND SHIPPERS 264

7.1 The Leads Surround You 264
7.2 Review Your Purchase History and Compare 265
7.3 Look at the Competition 265
7.4 Use MacRae's Blue Book and Other Shippers Lists 266
7.5 Livestock, Produce, and the USDA 267
7.6 Satellite View of Company Buildings 267
7.7 Cold Calling Shippers 268
7.8 Trust, Relationships, and Load Boards 269
7.9 Get Connected 269
7.10 Get What You Pay for 270
7.11 Get Quality Drivers by Being a Quality Broker 271

CHAPTER 8: THE LEGALITIES AND FORMALITIES 274

8.1 Freight Broker Compliance Requirements 274

CHAPTER 9: THE DAILY ROUTINE OF THE FREIGHT BROKER 280

CHAPTER 10: USING SOCIAL MEDIA TO GROW YOUR FREIGHT BROKING BUSINESS 286

10.1 Why use Social Media? 287
10.2 Facebook 288
10.3 Instagram 288
10.4 LinkedIn 289
10.5 Twitter 289

CONCLUSION 290

Book 1:

Operator Trucking Business Start-up

Introduction

The trucking industry is cyclically made up of companies that provide shipping services to customers, usually commercial businesses, using tractor-trailers. The majority of trucking companies own and operate their fleets. However, some companies also rely on leasing. Because international shipments require air or sea transportation, a large proportion of revenue is generated domestically. As a result, these businesses are relatively unaffected by currency fluctuations. The industry is certainly a good predictor of the overall economy. Customers begin to ship more goods during the early stages of an economic upswing in anticipation of better business conditions. A drop in trucking demand, on the other hand, could signal the start of a recession. This is a competitive industry. Customers can choose from various operators, including privately held carriers and non-industry companies such as air transporters. Consequently, day-to-day operations are primarily focused on relationships. To generate repeat sales, businesses strive to form close relationships with their customers. Customers can easily find a different shipper, so providing excellent service is a critical factor for the shippers. The price war is intense, and the companies in this group operate on razor-thin profit margins. A large trucking company must have owned a large collection of tractors and trailers, often in the thousands, to serve the needs of its customers adequately. Furthermore, the fleet must be upgraded regularly. The replacement period for tractors is usually five years. Because older vehicles require more maintenance, frequent upgrades help keep maintenance costs at a minimum. A young fleet may also attract better-qualified drivers, particularly when labor is limited. Furthermore, increasingly stringent environmental regulations in the United States force trucking companies to purchase newer and more fuel-efficient vehicles. Fleet sizes are frequently adjusted in response to changing economic conditions. Truckers will reduce the number of operating vehicles during downturns to avoid holding excess capacity. When the supply of tractors outnumbers the demand, less revenue is generated per vehicle. This also results in other inefficiencies. The trucking industry is separated into two categories: less-than-truckload (LTL) and truckload. The Truckload stands to load a trailer with large amounts of cargo from a single customer, usually for delivery to a single location. LTL drivers load a trailer with small amounts of cargo from several customers, all of whom require different delivery destinations. LTL shipments may stop at multiple terminals. LTL shipments are also transferred between multiple vehicles before arriving at their final destination. On the contrary, both types of trucking companies operate a nationwide network of terminals and distribution centers. Seasonal factors have an impact on the industry. In general, all trucking companies experience increased demand in the fourth quarter of the calendar year. It is the time when retailers stock the shelves in preparation for the busy holiday shopping season. Because there is less need to transport large amounts of homogeneous freight in the middle of the year, LTL companies may see higher demand than truckload companies. The first quarter is typically slow for both LTL and truckload carriers, which is a good thing because this time of year is primarily responsible for weather-related delays. Several significant expenses influence trucking companies' profitability. Earnings are heavily influenced by labor costs. A large number of qualified drivers and freight handlers are typically required by trucking companies. Because the supply of available drivers is often limited, there is fierce competition for qualified drivers. To attract the best employees, businesses must offer competitive wages and benefits. Some trucking companies employ members of powerful labor unions. These employees have significant bargaining power, and labor unrest is a possibility. Nonunion workers are less expensive to hire, but they may not be as dependable. Pension and workers' compensation costs are two other significant labor-related costs. Another expense that must be carefully managed is fuel. Tractor-trailer fuel consumption is high due to long trips, heavy loads, and large engines. Surcharges are used to pass on a large percentage of the cost of diesel fuel to customers. However, if fuel prices rise rapidly, it may take longer to recoup all related expenses, reducing a trucker's short-term profitability. Most businesses prefer surcharges over long-term fuel contract hedging. Based on the cost of each source, cash flow, common equity, and debt may be used to fund operational expansion and fleet improvements. Usually, mergers provide enhanced market coverage, but these come at the cost of heavy debt. In general, the stock market risk of these companies is average. Shippers and carriers benefit from transportation intermediaries' expertise, technological investments, and human resources. The services provided by brokers benefit both motor carriers and shippers. In exchange for a commission, they assist carriers in filling their trucks. They help shippers find dependable motor carriers. Some companies use brokers as their traffic department, allowing them to use the broker to coordinate all of their shipping and transportation management needs. Brokers have long been a part of the trucking industry, dating back to its inception in the early twentieth century. This book covers all topics and terms related to starting a trucking business. You will learn about the history of trucking, the evolution of the trucking industry, and regulations, and the impact on the trucking business. You will be able to master the trucking industry's terms and jargon and the different market strategies and tactics for thriving in the trucking business.

CHAPTER 1:

History of Trucks and Trucking Business

The truckers could easily be seen moving on the roads and highways. They are considered to be one of the most reliable and oldest modes of transporters. They transport items from one location to another. They also work different hours than regular employees. They also spend their nights driving on the roads. They try hard to deliver the shipment during business hours. Who is this person? We're discussing truckers and the trucking industry. Since Karl Benz installed the first internal combustion engine in a truck in the late 1800s, trucking has been a part of the transportation industry. Before this date, the trucks were driven by steam engines. The switch to an internal combustion engine improved truck performance. These engines were extremely powerful and could transport larger loads over longer distances, resulting in more efficient trucks. The trucking industry, like the automobile industry, has seen technological advancements. The engines became more powerful and efficient with time. For truck drivers, the cabs became more comfortable. Additionally, trailers improved, allowing truckers to transport virtually any load. In terms of how trucks and the trucking industry have progressed over time, the history of trucks and the trucking industry is fascinating. Gottlieb Daimler, a German automotive pioneer, built the first motor truck in 1896. Daimler's truck had a four-horsepower engine. The engine has a belt drive with two forward speeds. Moreover, the belt drive also has one reverse speed. It was the first pickup truck on the market. In 1885, Daimler developed the world's first motorcycle, and in 1897, the first taxi.

1.1 The First Tow Truck

The birth of towing industry took place in 1916 in Chattanooga, Tennessee, when Ernest Holmes, Sr., used three poles, a pulley, and a chain attached to the frame of a 1913 Cadillac to help a friend retrieve his car. Following the patenting of his invention, Holmes began producing wreckers and towing tools for sale to auto mechanics and anyone else interested in towing and retrieving disabled or wrecked vehicles. He established a small shop on Market Street. As the auto industry grew, Holmes' company grew, and its products secured a worldwide reputation for quality and performance. Ernest Holmes, Sr. died in 1943, and his son, Ernest Holmes, Jr., took over as president until his retirement in 1973. Later on, the company was purchased by the Dover Corporation. Gerald Holmes, the founder's grandson, left the company and started his own, Century Wreckers. He established a manufacturing facility near Ooltewah, Tennessee, and his hydraulically-powered wreckers quickly outperformed the original company.

Miller Industries eventually purchased both companies' assets, as well as the assets of other wrecker manufacturers. Miller has retained the Century facility in Ooltewah, which produces both Century and Holmes wreckers. Miller is also a manufacturer of Challenger wreckers.

1.2 Forklift Trucks

The American Society of Mechanical Engineers defines the industrial truck as a power-propelled truck, mobile that is used to push, carry, pull, stack, lift, or tier materials. Powered industrial trucks are also called pallet trucks, forklifts, rider trucks, forklift trucks.

The first forklift was created in 1906. Moreover, there has not been a major change in a forklift since its invention. Before the invention of the forklift, a system of chains was normally used to lift heavy objects.

1.3 Mack Trucks

Jack and Gus Mack established Mack Trucks, Inc. in 1900 in Brooklyn, New York. Mack Trucks was originally known as the Mack Brothers Company.

The British government purchased and employed the Mack AC model to transport food and equipment to its troops during World War I. Consequently, it was named "Bulldog Mack," which also created the company's logo as the bulldog.

1.4 Semi-Trucks

Alexander Winton of Cleveland, Ohio, invented the first semi-truck in 1898. Winton started as a car manufacturer. He needed a way to get his cars to buyers all over the country.

As a result of his passion, the semi was born – a massive truck with 18 wheels and three axles that could carry a lot of weight. The semi is steered by the front axle, while it is propelled forward by the rear axle and its double wheels.

1.5 The Emergence of Modern Trucking

Trucking had been completely established as an important part of the economy by the 1930s. The military had already used trucks in the First World War. Paved roads, on the other hand, drew new attention and prompted new regulations. The Interstate Highway System, which was built in the 1950s and 1960s to connect the country's major population centers, accelerated the growth of trucking. Some trucks began to use propane-powered refrigerated trailers, allowing for more efficient transportation of frozen goods. By the 1970s, trucking had gained cultural prominence. Many films and songs about trucking gained popularity during this decade and the one before it. During the 1970s energy crises, truckers played a key role in organizing strikes against rising fuel prices. Trucking had become an essential and integral part of the freight industry by the 1980s. The volume of cargo had increased to the point where truckers were on the road at all hours of the day. Trucking has also become a major factor in the success of big-box retailers such as Target and Wal-Mart. The number of goods transported increased exponentially after the establishment of these corporate networks. The Load bar was quickly developed to protect shipped goods from damage by blocking and bracing cargo. Pallets, crates, and other items were consequently secured more effectively. In addition, there was a continued focus on environmental awareness, fuel efficiency, and cost-effectiveness. Trucking, as we know it today, had finally emerged by that time.

CHAPTER 2:

What is a Trucking Business?

A person as an owner can start a trucking business with one truck. Moreover, a company can own thousands of trucks that many different drivers drive. According to the estimation of the United States, Labor Department a truck normally hauls approximately 70% of everything we wear, eat, use or enjoy around our home, in our school, or at our job. It is the truck that carries the pieces or raw materials from the suppliers to a manufacturer to facilitate them in creating or manufacturing products.

These are then carried to the store by the trucks from where we can buy for our living. The above can easily deciphered that making a trucking business work smoothly is quite a challenge.

2.1 Why do we need the trucking industry?

Goods and products must be transported from their origin to points throughout the country, including each state, city, and suburb. A product's demand is confirmed whenever an order is placed online. This means that a product has to be manufactured and shipped. A factory owner will call a trucking company from the office to tell them what needs to be picked up, where it needs to be delivered, and when it needs to be delivered. They process the paperwork to guide the driver to the appropriate location. Every employee in a trucking company is essential. Each member of the mechanic, administration, loader, safety person, dispatcher, and trucker plays an equally important role in the entire process.

2.2 Employment

According to Business Insider, approximately 800,000 truck drivers are employed in the United States' trucking industry. Moreover, their collective yearly income is around US$30 billion. The owner-operator model, in which the truck driver is self-employed, is common in small trucking businesses. Larger trucking companies commonly employ union drivers. Unions work to protect the interests of drivers, similar to trucking associations which work to safeguard the interests of the entire industry. The International Brotherhood of Teamsters, for instance, is a powerful labor union with massive economic power and influence. The economy could easily come to a halt by a large-scale strike. This could also result in shipping delays and massive price increases because retailers try to keep up with consumer demand.

2.3 Essential details

The operations manager directs the dispatcher to enter data on the computer complete necessary paperwork after factoring in the following:

- The final price is set after incorporating special fees for fast and quick delivery

- Provision of a team of truck drivers for the safe and timely delivery
- Additional cost to cover higher fuel prices

2.4 Basics of trucking business

We've all heard stories about truckers who don't make it past their first year.

When they learn to drive, they are not taught how to establish a small trucking company. They make mistakes that cause them to lose their trucks, suffer significant financial losses, and possibly harm their families. It's difficult to watch as a newcomer struggles to run a successful trucking company and ends up in worse shape than when they began.

This is a once-in-a-lifetime opportunity for many new truckers. Without a doubt, trucking is one of the best ways to start a business. However, if this new owner-operator lacks basic business knowledge, it will take a long to establish a successful trucking business.

2.5 Important considerations

An owner-operator must know the following key facts if he wants to run a successful trucking company.

Gain experience

You can master the field of trucking after acquiring sufficient knowledge and experience. You must consult the truckers who have experience driving thousands of miles on trucks and learn their secrets. The sole objective is not to learn how to carry a load. The target should be to drive your truck long-term.

You must understand business basics

The principles of accounting, fundamentals of management, and marketing strategies can be learned in a variety of ways. You must understand how those business fundamentals apply to trucking to succeed as an owner-operator or freight broker. You'll almost certainly never hear about the IFTA or IRP if you take a bookkeeping or accounting class. You'll need to know a lot more than you'll learn in a class about trucking accounting. All businesses must follow management rules. Although managing a truck stop differs from managing an owner-operator business, the fundamentals remain the same.

You must gain an insight into the working of the trucking industry

You should be curious and intelligent enough to know about the future demands of your present and prospective customers.

On top of that, you should devise a way of fulfilling your customers' needs in a much better way than your competitors. You should be able to identify customers who could give you repeat business. The most important task would be to retain your customers in the long-run

Since you are an entrepreneur, you must know the difference between revenue and profit

It means that before you put money in your pocket, you subtract your expenses. You must set aside funds for a rainy day. It entails keeping your state and federal tax authorities informed. Basic writing and interpersonal skills are also advantageous.

You must develop an avid understanding of the trucking business

These skills can be learned through classes or by reading books and watching free educational videos online. You don't have to waste your free time on your laptop watching stupid TV programs. You can find a wealth of useful information on the internet. You'll discover the appropriate software tools which all truckers must use right now. It is worth remembering that the trucking industry is far too complicated to operate without computers. You must keep track of more information and data than ever before.

2.6 Difference between an owner-operator and company driver

Details don't matter when you're just a driver. When you're the owner-operator, everything counts. If you want to learn everything there is to know about establishing and operating a successful trucking company; you'll need the right software.

2.7 Why you should start a trucking company business

For a variety of reasons, establishing and operating a trucking company today can be extremely rewarding. It's because starting a trucking company is simpler than you might think. The logistics industry is currently experiencing a 75,000-truck shortage, with up to 200,000 trucks needed by the end of 2021. An estimated 10 to 20 full truck loads are to be moved for every single truck on the highway today, and the demand for trucks to move freight will continue to grow as the economy grows. The advantages of owning a trucking company without having to buy one are listed below.

Starting a trucking business makes you money

In today's America, a trucking company's business is a surefire way to make money. You can see income generated immediately for every full truck load moved. It's worth noting that you get paid the moment you get a load, so there's not much time to wait in between. The value of each truck load is based on the type of trailer your truck is towing. Moreover, your payments are linked with the miles covered by you. For example, if you're hauling building materials on a flatbed for 2000 miles, your truck could earn up to US$8000.00. As a result, it's critical to choose the right trailer for moving freight and ensure that your driver can handle it. There are different types of trailers that can be used to transport freight in the transportation industry. Flatbed trailers generate the maximum income, and they are followed by refrigerated trailers. Although general box freight pays less, the amount of freight available is limitless. By owning any of these types of trailers with their trucking company, a person can make anywhere from $50,000 to $75,000 per year and keep their truck moving daily. Because your company is new, you will be constrained to getting freight for the first six months of your new trucking company. Working with a freight broker who can assist you in getting dispatched and finding consistent freight is critical. Freight brokers are in charge of coordinating with numerous different shippers. Freight brokers will help you to start hauling freight as a new trucking company. As your time in business grows, more shippers will begin to give you freight after a few months of operating with your federal authority. Regardless of how new their trucking business is; anyone can keep it moving freight daily with the help of a good freight broker. Moreover, it is imperative for you, as a beginner owner-operator, to reach out to a freight broker in the early stages of your business to explicitly communicate to him the freight your truck will be hauling.

Starting a trucking company is affordable

If you are determined to start a new trucking company, it will cost you about $1200.00. This is normally the cost of your filings, but some states have different fees, so check with a consulting firm to determine what you'll be paying. One of your responsibilities would be to apply for the federal MC and DOT numbers. This will cost you approximately $300.00. After registering with the FMCSA, you'll need to apply for a UCR filing and an IFTA account to transport freight across numerous states. A professional firm can handle these filings that will file on your behalf, ensuring that no errors are made and that the authority is granted within 21 days of your filing date. Before your MC Authority can grant you an Active status, the FMCSA requires you to wait 21 days. The final requirement is that you have a $750,000 liability insurance policy added to your MC Authority. It is only after fulfilling your liability insurance policy that the FMCSA will allow you to move freight.

The following are the required filings to initiate your own trucking company:

USDOT Number

This number is provided by the U.S. Department of Transportation (DOT). It collects and keeps track of your company's safety information, inspections, crash investigations, etc.

Operating Authority

To transport freight over state borders, all for-hire carriers must get permission from the DOT. Your authority also specifies the kinds of freight you may transport.

Heavy Vehicle Use Tax

Heavy vehicle use tax is charged on all trucks that weigh more than 55,000 pounds.

International Registration Plan (IRP)

IRP breaks down registration fees among states and provinces in the United States and Canada based on distance traveled. You must register on the transportation website of your state.

International Fuel Tax Agreement (IFTA)

IFTA is an agreement between the lower 48 states of the United States and the provinces of Canada to make it easy to report fuel used by carriers who travel between states.

Carriers submit a quarterly fuel tax report that calculates and distributes their tax to the states. You need to have an IFTA decal on your truck, and you must apply for a new one at the start of each year.

BOC-3 Filing

In each state where you have an office or have contracts, you must designate a process agent. This is the name of your company's process agent. The process agent is the person who acts on your behalf, and all the legal proceedings are also served to him. After these filings are completed, you can expect to wait anywhere from 21 to 30 days for your first load. For the first year, the FMCSA will enroll you in the New Trucking Entrant Program, and you will be required to meet with a DOT inspector for your first safety audit. This enables anyone to begin learning the requirement. This also simplifies your audit procedure's completion. Several companies can assist you in learning and keeping your new trucking company compliant with FMCSA guidelines, as well as preparing for the safety audit.

Be an owner Operator-There is no need to own a truck to start a trucking business

As previously stated, the volume of freight available in the trucking industry is virtually limitless, which is excellent news for trucking company owners. The majority of people believe they need to purchase a truck, which can be costly.

The truth is that you do not have to be the truck and trailer's owner. You only need to be the trucking company's owner. Using another person's truck and trailer to start a new trucking company is possible. This is an owner-operator, and the owner-operator truck can be registered under your authority. The owner-operator would be a lease-on driver for you. The driver will be driving his truck and trailer for you. This method would allow you to earn around $500.00 per week or more, and many people are finding it profitable to embrace this type of trucking business model. Insurance companies typically allow you to have three to four trucks under your new Federal MC Authority for the first year. You should be cognizant that you are being watched to ensure that you are operating your trucking business following the new Trucking Entrant Program. You will be able to generate approximately US $2000 every week by keeping four trucks under your trucking company. After your first year, insurance underwriters will start allowing you to add more trucks to your Federal MC Authority. Thus they would allow you to grow your new trucking business organically. After the first year, it is recommended that you purchase your first truck and trailer, as this will increase your weekly income by an additional $1000.00.

You can work from home with your trucking business

Today, owning a trucking company does not necessitate having a large trucking facility. The majority of people who start their own trucking company do so from their own homes. Your truck transports freight daily, usually over the road, and you only see it when performing maintenance or checking your equipment. GPS location software allows you to keep track of your truck's activities from the comfort of your own home. This enables you to work from home and dispatch your truck with full truck loads daily. For the first year, you can also save money by permitting a freight broker to dispatch your truck while you focus on keeping your company compliant with FMCSA regulations. A computer and a phone are the most basic requirements for dispatching your truck. If you own a trucking company but don't have your trucks, you'll only need a home office for dispatching as well as monitoring your business. All you'd need is a basic computer with load board software and a TMS (Transportation Management Software). The truck driver sends you the information, along with documents, electronically from within the cab about the freight load delivery. To get paid for the load, you upload your documents and send them in for funding. After delivering your freight load, you can usually expect to be paid within a few days. The TMS software also handles basic truck reporting and accounting, and everything you need to run your trucking company can be done virtually from your home office. This is the daily routine that can be followed by in your trucking business. This also helps you to ensure that your driver completes their truck inspection reports every week and that your trucking company continues to grow. If you work with a freight broker, they will send you daily reports of the loads that have been moved. You will then enter these reports into your TMS software. With only one or two trucks on the road moving freight, you might expect to work a few hours a day from your home office. Working from home and running your own trucking company can be extremely rewarding and provide you with a good income. Countless freight brokers who start their own freight brokerage company also own a trucking company. By combining the two businesses, you have a fantastic opportunity to start a serious home business in logistics.

2.8 Regulation Costs

Regulation, according to studies, increased costs as well as rates significantly. Without regulation, not only was it rated lower, but service quality was also better as judged by shippers. Products exempt from regulation moved at 20 to

40% lower rates than those subject to ICC controls. When comparing heavily regulated trucking in West Germany and the United States to unregulated motor carriage in the US and lightly regulated trucking in the Netherlands and Belgium, it was discovered that charges in heavily regulated countries were 75 percent higher than charges in countries with more open markets.

The Motor Carrier Act (MCA) of 1980

The Motor Carrier Act (MCA) of 1980 only deregulated trucking to a limited extent. However, when combined with a liberal ICC, it effectively freed the industry. The MCA made obtaining a certificate of public convenience and necessity for a trucker much easier. The MCA also required the commission to remove most restrictions on the commodities that could be transported and restrictions on the routes that motor carriers could take and the geographic areas they could serve.

The Success of Deregulation

Deregulation has proven to be effective. Rates for truckload-size shipments fell about 25% in real, inflation-adjusted terms between 1977 before the ICC began deregulating the industry and 1982. The General Accounting Office discovered that LTL (less-than-truckload) carrier rates had dropped by as much as 10% to

20%, with some shippers reporting declines of up to 40%. Between 1979 and 1986, revenue per truckload ton fell by 22%. According to a survey of shippers, service quality has improved as well. Deregulation of trucking was favored by 77 percent of shippers as per a survey conducted during that period. Before deregulation, shippers reported that carriers were much more ready to bargain rates and services.

Savings

One of the major benefits of trucking deregulation to the economy has been a significant reduction in the cost of holding and maintaining inventories. As a result, inventories have become comparatively lean. Manufacturers could indeed order components just in time for use, and retailers can have them just in time to sell because truckers are better able to provide on-time delivery and more flexible service. These changes would not have been possible without the partial deregulation which resulted from the 1980 act.

CHAPTER 3:

Getting Started

There are many things that you must know before you attempt to start a trucking company.

3.1 What to know before you start

Given below are the top things that you must know before starting a trucking company.

Have an emergency cash reserve?

This is undoubtedly the most common reason behind new businesses' fail. It's not uncommon for a motivated individual to enter the transportation industry as a leased driver and become a leased owner-operator. Trucking is a lucrative business. At the same time, the profit margins are extremely low. As Benjamin Franklin famously said, you must watch the pennies, and the dollars will take care of themselves. This is fantastic advice. This necessitates the creation of an emergency reserve. Murphy's Law states, "If anything can go wrong, it will." This is especially true in the trucking industry. Truckers are vulnerable to a variety of catastrophes. The operator could face everything from DOT officer shakedowns to tire blowouts to broker scams. As a result, it is highly recommended to keep a cash reserve of 60-90 days for challenging and difficult situations.

Trucking is not for the weak

You can find a score of ambitious people who start a trucking business with a truck and a dream to excel but without any planning. The truck and the dream will be gone before you know it. No general can win a battle without making any calculation or doing any planning. To be successful in trucking, you need a lot more than a truck and a CDL. Several people have no idea how to figure out their base operating cost per mile.

Furthermore, they are unaware that variable costs per mile calculations exist.

The 3 new best friends you need right now

You have to identify and make your three new best friends without any delay. The three new friends are:

Bookkeeper or accountant

You direly need the services of an experienced transportation accounting specialist. You must not waste your time and try to hire the services of an experienced bookkeeper! Seriously, it's very critical for your overall success. There's simply too much going on out on the road. So you need to have the services of an expert for proper bookkeeping. Plus, we know you could save money by having your spouse do it for you. This is not a good idea. You can cut corners in many areas, but this one will put your business out of business if you make a mistake.

Safety & Compliance Consultant

There are now several attorneys who can provide legal and compliance advice and safety consulting services. We'll say it right now: the government does not support trucking companies. The Department of Transportation (DOT) and the Federal Motor Carrier Safety Administration (FMCSA) are government-run agencies tasked with policing the transportation industry. When in doubt, the rules will prioritize the needs of the general public over the interests of trucking companies. We desire trucking companies to operate safely; it's a reasonable expectation. However, we are approaching the point where you will need someone, if not a team, on your side to deal with government oversight and regulations. This is what your lawyer does. The core task of the lawyer is to safeguard your company's and your rights. Now, more than ever, you require the services of a trucking attorney. There isn't much room for error. The Department of Transportation will cancel your authorization on a single non-compliance. You're doomed if you hire a bad driver. If you do not manage and adhere to safety principles, then you will be done with your trucking business in no time.

Insurance Agent

Many agents claim to be able to provide you with a free insurance quote. This, indeed, is correct. There are even a few agents who are solely focused on trucking insurance. After the insurance is bound, the essential thing for trucking companies is SERVICE. Is your agent willing to give you access to the certificate 24 hours a day, 7 days a week? After 5:00 p.m., many brokers book urgent loads that pay the best.

What will you do if your agent is unavailable for the day? How do they deal with insurance claims and policy changes? Is there any person who can handle phone calls and resolve the issues for you?

Know your Options

Following are some of the options that you must be aware of. You have to think about these options before you decide to start spending money on anything.

Option 1

Whether you want to stay as a driver or become an owner-operator, the choice is yours. This may appear ridiculous, but it is a viable option to consider. aDo you think you've got what it takes to run your own business? Your best decision could be to continue working as a professional driver. However, in most situations, you would be much better off and would be able to generate more money if you find the right company to work with. This could help you earn a substantial amount, increase stability, and happier home life.

Option 2

It would help if you always went for a corporate company. You have to make a decision and select between the sole proprietor, S-Corp, C-Corp, LLC. Each has its own advantages ande disadvantages. For a wise decision, you would need the services of an attorney.

Option 3

If you research the new MC Authority, you'll find hundreds of pages of companies offering to complete your FMCSA/DOT Authority Licensing application for various fees. It would be best if you determined which service provider is best for you.

Option 4

You have to select an insurance /agent to post your insurance filings and service your insurance contract for the next 12 months. This underscores the importance of hiring the services of an agent.

Option 5

So you've decided not to lease to another trucking company, which leaves you with the following options: A. Hire a dispatcher or B.

Be your dispatcher. This is an informed decision. It is because the improper dispatcher/brokers could very well put you out of business before you could even make additional truck payments.

Know Your Trucking Success Formula

The formula MILES = $$$ is the guiding factor in trucking. Money, on the other hand, is not synonymous with success. Money isn't everything when it comes to success. Success is defined differently by each person and has different connotations.

However, for many in the trucking industry, success means having more time with their families or leaving a financial legacy.

The important thing is to start with the end in mind. If you are not aware of your destination or objectives, it would be a daunting task for you to draw a destination map if you don't know where you're going.

Furthermore, starting with a mental picture of the end goal is self-defeating if that goal turns out not to be what you thought you wanted.

3.2 Getting Started-Guide to how to start a trucking business

The trucking industry is heavily regulated. There is a score of government requirements you'll need to meet and keep up with before your business can start operating. If you want to initiate a trucking company right now, here's a step-by-step guide that will help you do so quickly and strategically.

This will assist you in starting your new trucking company and realizing your dream of owning your own trucking company.

Anyone interested in learning how to start a trucking company will find information here that will serve as a guide to establishing a reliable trucking company in today's logistics market.

3.3 A complete guide to starting a new trucking company

Given below is the step-by-step process for starting a new trucking company.

Buy or lease a truck and trailer

You can buy or lease equipment in the same way that you can buy or lease vehicles. In either case, you must first determine the type of freight you intend to transport. Do you intend to run day trips only, or will you require a sleeper cabin? Will you buy a van, a flatbed trailer, or a refrigerated trailer as your first trailer? The following are some of the most popular types of leases:

Operating (Full-Service) Lease

This lease allows you to handle maintenance, taxes, and permits. Moreover, you can easily quit at the end of the lease term.

Terminal Rental Adjustment Clause (TRAC) Lease

You may make a minimal down payment with this lease. You may purchase the vehicle at its book value after the term. You may also delegate the sale of the vehicle to the leasing firm. You receive the profit if the leasing firm makes the money on the sale. You must, however, pay the difference if the leasing firm loses money.

Lease-Purchase Plans

Truckers who have bad credit or do not have sufficient funds for a down payment should look into lease-purchase plans. According to experts, you will usually pay more in such schemes than you would in traditional financing.

Get driving experience

You must first obtain a commercial driver's license (CDL). You can enroll in a private truck driving school, or some trucking companies could sponsor you to attend a CDL school through their training programs. Many drivers who become owner-operators started as company drivers and gained rich experience in truck driving.

Develop a business plan

You have to have a business plan before initiating your trucking company business. That should clearly show how much money you'll make and how much money you'll spend. Remember to include the money that will be paid to you for your livelihood. You might want to employ a business consultant to help you figure out which plan is best for you.

Save money to cover start-up expenses

You must be aware that initiating a trucking company requires a significant upfront investment in the form of a tractor and trailer(s) and licensing and registration requirements. Identify financing sources and terms, as well as secure a line of credit. Experts advise having sufficient cash in reserves to cover the first six months of business expenses, including lease payments.

Plan your business operations

You have to plan the business operations of your trucking company. You must be aware of the important issues like:

- Where will you park the truck/equipment?
- Truck maintenance issues
- Sales strategy for finding loads
- Who will handle the invoices, accounting, payroll, and taxes?

3.4 Obtain a trucking business license

The first step in starting a trucking company is to establish a legal trucking company in your state. You should choose a name that reflects your company's mission.

You should also file the required documents with your state. We recommend that you use Incorporate.com to help you with your business filing, which can be completed in a matter of days. You should also apply for an EIN (Employer Identification Number). Without an EIN, you won't be able to move forward. You also have to ensure the accuracy of the EIN information, just like your business information. You'll decide which entity is best for forming your trucking company. We recommend forming a limited liability company (LLC). Your options are:

- Sole proprietorship
- Partnership
- Limited liability corporation (LLC)
- Corporation (C-corp, S-corp, etc.)

3.5 Permits and licenses for operating a trucking company

The trucking industry is heavily regulated. It can be difficult to go through myriad government regulations that apply to trucking companies. To operate, a trucking company must pay special taxes and obtain special permits from the federal and state governments, as well as have CDLs (Commercial Driver's Licenses) and any other permits that may be required, such as a HazMat (Hazardous Materials) certification. Before the permission for pulling out of the trucking company yard with a HazMat load, drivers who haul chemical solvents or other dangerous substances must take special classes and have the certification on their CDL.

There are also plenty of government requirements you'll need to meet and keep up with before your business can start operating. Given below are the steps to facilitate you to secure your authority and operate legally as an interstate trucking company.

3.6 Get a Commercial Driver's License

All of your company's drivers must have valid commercial driver's licenses as they are required for operating heavy trucks (CDLs). A detailed background check, a written permit exam, CDL training, and a driving test are all required to obtain a license. You have to be at least 18 years old to apply for a CDL. To drive a truck from one state to another, you should be at least 21 years old. For CDLs, each state has its own set of requirements. Pick up a CDL manual from the local Department of Motor Vehicles office to determine what your state requires.

Apply for EIN Employer Identification Number

Federal EIN could be applied online with the IRS.

You have to ensure to provide the same information as was furnished with your business license. https://www.irs.gov/businesses/small-businesses-self-employed/apply-for-an-employer-identification-number-ein-online

Apply for your US DOT and MC Operating Authority

You can initiate the procedure for acquiring your MC Authority online. For this, you have to get your trucking company business registered through the URS (Unified

Registration System). The address of the website portal is. (https://portal.fmcsa.dot.gov/UrsRegistrationWizard/)

You will be asked to create an account with the URS once you start the registration process. For access to the application, FMCSA would like you to create an account. If you cannot complete your application in one go, your account would then allow you to return to finish it later. The FMCSA will assign you an Applicant ID. You'll be prompted to create a password and propose security questions. You will receive an MC# and a USDOT# as a result of the application process. You will receive a PIN # emailed to your business address, which will allow you to log into your FMCSA Accounts. Since you can get a duplicate pin only through the mail, you must keep this PIN safe and secure. Your USDOT Number is a number issued by the United States Department of Transportation (DOT). The USDOT Number is used to collect and track your company's safety data, inspections, and crash investigations. Your MC Operating Authority is for-hire. Therefore, the carriers must obtain permission from the Department of Transportation to transport freight across state lines. Your authority also defines the types of freight you are allowed to transport.

Apply for your UCR Filing

The UCR ACT was established in 2005. It only addresses those motor carriers, freight brokers, and freight forwarders who do business to profit. The fleet size of the trucking company determines the annual fee. At the same time, the freight brokers and freight forwarders are only charged the minimum fee. The UCR is used to fund and maintain state highways, as well as safety programs. UCR fees are calculated based on a carrier's total number of vehicles. Vehicles do not include trailers. The number of self-propelled commercial motor vehicles reported on the carrier's most recent Form MCS-150 filed with the FMCSA is the number of commercial motor vehicles used to calculate carrier UCR fees. Visit the LFS Guide to UCR Filing for more information on UCR filing. If you need to file for a UCR, you must fit into one of five categories. If your trucking company falls into one of the five categories, you must apply for a UCR.

- Operations that require an MC or MX number from the FMCSA
- Interstate brokers
- Operations that require a USDOT number for interstate transportation
- Interstate leasing companies
- Interstate freight forwarders

Apply for Trucking Liability Insurance

One of the most important things for your trucking company is Liability Insurance. Furthermore, you are not allowed to open a trucking company without liability insurance. The FMCSA will give you approximately 21 days from the date of filing your MC Authority and DOT application to apply for Liability Insurance with the FMCSA Authority Application. The minimum liability insurance limit is $750,000, but many new trucking companies go for a policy limit of $1,000,000. The FMCSA does not mandate this level of liability insurance. However, the majority of shippers opt for the said. It is preferable to have the liability insurance that the shipper requests as this will improve your freight options.

The following is a list of the various insurance policies that the trucking company should concentrate on when it initiates its trucking business:

- Primary Liability: At least $750,000 in primary liability coverage.
- Cargo: $100,000
- Physical Damage:
- Non-Trucking Use (Bobtail)

Obtain a process agent and file a form BOC-3

He is the person who works as a process agent. He is either your trucking company's representative or freight broker's representative who may be served legal papers on your behalf. This is typically needed by state law in the United States and is also referred to as a registered agent, a resident agent, or a statutory agent. All freight forwarders, trucking companies, and freight broker companies must have a process agent in 50 states. This is a prerequisite by the FMCSA. A BOC-3 form is used to file the documents.

Register for an IFTA Account

You cannot register the IFTA account and IRP Portion Plates until granting active status to your trucking authority. The FMCSA will send Your Trucking Authority Certificate to your registered business address by the FMCSA within 21 days of your filing. Another prerequisite for completing the process is the availability of your trucking liability insurance policy as well. There is an agreement among the lower 48 U.S. states and Canadian provinces called the International Fuel Tax Agreement (IFTA). This agreement simplifies the procedure for reporting fuel consumption by carriers who drive in multiple states. The couriers file a quarterly fuel tax report. This report determines their tax and distributes it to the states. The truck must have an IFTA decal on it. Moreover, application for a new account is mandatory at the beginning of every year. Trucking Company should have the capability for additional filings for IFTA in other States as well.

Or in other States, as required IN New Mexico

A New Mexico weight distance tax account is required for all motor carriers who operate vehicles in New Mexico with a gross vehicle weight of more than 26,000 pounds. The trucking company must file three monthly reports once the account is opened. This is another precondition along with that of the IFTA license.

Kentucky

Weight distance tax applies to all motor carriers that operate in Kentucky with a total weight of sixty thousand pounds or more. A KYU account is required for such carriers. After the opening of the account, it becomes mandatory to file quarterly reports. On their truck, the motor carrier is not bound to display the KYU number. Your USDOT number is used to verify vehicles. However, any change in the trucks' inventory list is to be updated and reported to Kentucky. This is another requirement along with the IFTA license.

New York

A weight distance tax, New York Highway Tax (HUT), is charged from all carriers operating in motor vehicles with over 18,000 pounds on New York highways. Opening of a HUT account and registration of each vehicle that travels in New York is also mandatory. This is another requirement along with the IFTA license.

Oregon

All carriers with a cumulative vehicle weight of more than 26,000 pounds are subject to the Oregon Highway Use Tax. This is known as a mileage tax. If you are planning to travel through Oregon, you'll need an Oregon Weight Receipt as well as a Tax Identifier Receipt. To open an account in Oregon, you'll also need to file a bond. Once you've secured the account, you'll be required to submit monthly reports. Mileage tax is the only tax that Oregon charges, and it does not levy a fuel tax.

File for International Registration Plan (IRP)

The IRP distributes the registration fees based on distance traveled in each U.S. state or Canadian province. It would help if you got registered on your state's transportation website. You can contact your local DMV (Department of Motor Vehicles) for assistance in finding an IRP registration location near you. IRP is also known as Apportioned Registration. IRP is used for the registration of fleets of vehicles that move between multiple member jurisdictions. The plan includes all 50 states (except for Alaska and Hawaii) and ten Canadian provinces. IRP-eligible motor carriers must register their fleets of vehicles in their home or "base" jurisdiction. For the IRP, a fleet is composed of one or multiple trucks.

Apply for a SCAC Code (Standard Carrier Alpha Codes)

A Standard Carrier Alpha Code (SCAC) is a two- to four-letter code that transport companies use for their identification. A SCAC Code is required by all US federal agencies, numerous commercial shippers such as the automotive, petroleum, forest products, and chemical sectors, and suppliers to retail companies and ocean container drayage carriers and railroad piggyback trailers. Carriers that utilize the Uniform Intermodal Interchange Agreement (UIIA) must have a valid SCAC. SCACs are used in integrated software programs.

The petroleum industry uses these programs to speed up the motion of bills of lading, inventory data, and pipeline tickets. SCACs are used by numerous receivers and commercial shippers in the freight bill audit as well as payment systems. The NMFTA created the SCAC identification codes in the mid-1960s to help the transportation industry with computerization.

Visit https://secure.nmfta.org/Welcome.aspx to apply for a SCAC code.

Understanding ongoing compliance with the FMCSA

After the initiation of the process meant for the start of the new trucking company and permission from the FMCSA in the form of active status, you'll want to get started right away, following the FMCSA's guidelines. Within the first 10 to 18 months of your trucking company's launch, your trucking company will be entered into the new trucking entrant program, and you will be audited. The audit will ensure that you have been complying with the FMCSA's rules and regulations. At this stage, it is worth mentioning for the interest of new starters that FMCSA is very strict when it comes to compliance with its rules and standards. There is a zero-tolerance policy against trucking companies that fail to comply with FMCSA rules. Moreover, it charges severe penalties and fines. It is also mandatory to operate your trucking company under these guidelines from the start. We would recommend partnering with a consulting firm. The company will walk you through the process of starting a trucking company, implementing compliance, and securing your first load. With the right guidance, you can start your trucking company on the right foot.

Ultimately you will find a trucking business more lucrative than other businesses.

3.7 Business structure and documentation

The profit-generating potential of a trucking company is comparatively very high. Moreover, this business has the potential to post steady growth and also carries less risk. All new trucking company owners want to achieve the following objectives:

- Protection of personal assets
- To have tax options that enhance their bottom line
- Expand their business
- Establish credibility with their customers

All the objectives mentioned above can be achieved by forming a limited liability company (LLC.) Although each business is different, the ultimate right choice for any company should be to form an LLC. A trucking company can hire independent contractors to drive their trucks. It can also hire truckers as employees, which will result in higher profits and employee loyalty. However, this is to be kept in mind that hiring truckers increases overhead costs. To determine which hiring model is best for them, a trucking company owner must compare the costs and benefits of the two options. When deciding whether or not to form an LLC, trucking company owners must consider the following factors:

- Risk level
- Profit potential
- Credibility
- Consumer trust

Risk and limited liability

If a truck driver is injured on the job or injures someone by accident, trucking companies may face a personal injury lawsuit. There's also the possibility of causing damage to someone else's assets. An employee, for instance, damages a customer's building with a forklift during a merchandise offload. Any business that poses a risk to its owner must be legally separated from the owner. Limited liability protection is the term for this separation. If a company defaults or is sued, then the only remedy available to the owner for protecting his assets like car, house, and savings is limited liability.

Profit and LLC Taxes

A trucking company's average profit margin is approximately 6%. Providing flexible tax options through an LLC can prove extremely advantageous for a trucking company that earns a consistent profit. LLC owners have the option of paying taxes as a pass-through entity or as an S corporation (S corp). For businesses with less profit, pass-through taxation is best. Conversely, an S Corp is ideal for businesses that need to carry significant profit every year.

LLC vs. Corporation

The formation and maintenance of an LLC or corporation provide limited liability protection. But how do you know which business structure is best for your trucking firm? Only business owners who need to depend largely on outside investors should form a corporation. This is because of variations in taxation policies. If outside investors are important, a trucking company could very well gain financially by forming a corporation. The trucking companies which do not require outside investors can enjoy tax benefits by forming an LLC.

Credibility and consumer trust

Reliance on customer trust along with repeat purchases is what benefits the trucking companies. If you have established your credibility in your customers' eyes, it will help you run your business successfully. Businesses forming LLCs manage to enhance consumer trust and credibility.

3.8 Start-up costs for an owner-operator

This is the best time for you to begin your career as an owner-operator. Given the rising freight demand, the ongoing driver shortage, and increasing rates, this could be an excellent time to start a new trucking company. But you must be aware of the cost that is required to start a trucking company, though? Here's a breakdown of some of the most substantial expenses you'll face upon initiating a new trucking company.

The initial cost for starting a trucking business

Starting a trucking company can cost anywhere from $6,000 to $15,000 in the beginning. The said cost does not include the equipment cost. It includes costs related to documents required for registration and formation. These expenses range between $900 and $1,500 on average. IRP plates can range in price from $500 to $3,000 per truck. A permit and the Heavy Vehicle Use Tax can cost anywhere from $100 per truck to $600 per truck. You might also need to add a state-specific tax, which might be around $500 per truck on average. Truck drivers can make 30.3 cents per mile or about $32,000 per year on average. According to the US Bureau of Labor Statistics, the median annual wage for all occupations as of May 2017 was

$37,690. Vehicle transportation companies make a substantial profit of about 4.8 cents per operating dollar spent. Some drivers, however, may generate comparatively more earnings. This situation will indeed favor smaller businesses that want to launch their business with minimum capital investment.

On the other hand, a large-scale trucking company may require an investment of approximately $5 million in the beginning. When it comes to starting your own trucking company, you should always focus on committing minimum investment. You can start with just one unit, reducing your initial investment to a manageable level.

Fixed and variable costs ongoing costs of running a trucking company

You've successfully achieved the following targets:

- Initiated your trucking company
- Have received your authority
- Have all the permits needed to operate the trucking company
- The trucking company is all set to haul freight

This is time that you give due consideration to your operational costs. You must know the various types of costs. This initial knowledge will help you in anticipating expenses and setting a budget for your company. The startup costs are usually a blend of fixed costs and variable costs. For example, fixed costs might include the price of your truck unit, periodic maintenance, annual permits, taxes, and insurance costs. On the other hand, fuel costs, multifarious repair costs, and fines could make up your variable costs. For understanding, you must know that approximately 60-70% of the operating costs come from variable costs.

Fixed Costs

Fixed costs, like monthly insurance payments, monthly truck payments, and bi-weekly payroll are expenses that occur regularly. Permit or license renewals must be paid on an annual basis. Because these payments are usually the same and are not subject to any change, budgeting for them is usually straightforward.

Variable Costs

Variable costs fluctuate depending on how your trucking company is run. Fuel, maintenance and repairs, meals, and lodging make up the variable costs. After all, in the trucking industry, you can't make money without spending some. It is difficult to predict variable costs in contrast to fixed costs. You will not be able to assess your variable costs but only after a few months of operations.

Cost per mile (CPM)

The cost per mile is the operating cost for every mile you drive. It's calculated by dividing the costs by the number of miles you drive. You should be at home in calculating the cost per mile as this assists you in quoting and accepting a minimum freight rate at the time of booking loads. It would be worthwhile for the new operators to know that the average cost per mile, as reported by the American Trucking Research Institute (ATRI), was $1.65 in 2019.

Operating Ratio

This allows you to analyze your profit potential as well as monitor your losses. It's calculated by dividing the expense figure by the revenue figure.

Acquiring the US DOT number

A US DOT number is a must before you can start your trucking business. You could secure an MC / US DOT number against payment of $300.

Business registration

It would help if you got your business registered as a new owner-operator. The business registration cost usually varies from state to state. An average business registration cost of $500 could be incurred when starting your trucking business company.

A comprehensive breakdown of the business registration cost in each state

When you form a company in one state and then move to another state and do business there, you'll be required to register in both states. This necessitates the payment of state filing fees and taxes. It is a known fact that most small business owners gain an advantage by incorporating or forming an LLC in their home state. It's always useful to compare prices in all 50 states. Given below is a summary of each state's formation and annual maintenance fees.

Alabama

LLC filing fees: $165; LLC Annual Report; $0, Incorporation filing fees: $165; Corporation Annual Report: $0

Alaska

LLC filing fees: $250; LLC Initial Report: $0; LLC Annual Report: $100; Incorporation filing fees: $250; Corporation Initial Report: $0; Corporation Annual Report: $100

Arizona

LLC filing fees: $50; LLC Publication fee: $299 (required); LLC Annual Report: $0; Incorporation filing fees: $60; Corporation Publication fee: $299 (required); Corporation Annual Report: $45

Arkansas

LLC filing fees: $50; LLC Annual Report: $150; Incorporation filing fees: $50; Corporation Annual Report: $150

California

LLC filing fees: $75; LLC Initial Report $20; LLC Annual Report: $20; Incorporation filing fees: $105; Corporation Initial Report: $25; Corporation Annual Report: $25

Colorado

LLC filing fees: $50; LLC Annual Report: $10; Incorporation filing fees: $50; Corporation Annual Report: $10

Connecticut

LLC filing fees: $175; LLC Annual Report: $20; Incorporation filing fees: $455; Corporation Annual Report: $100

District of Columbia

LLC filing fees: $220; LLC Annual Report: $300; Incorporation filing fees: $220; Corporation Annual Report: $300

Delaware

LLC filing fees: $140; LLC Annual Report: $300; Incorporation filing fees: $140; Corporation Annual Report: $225 (based on min number of authorized shares)

Florida
LLC filing fees: $155; LLC Annual Report: $138.75; Incorporation filing fees: $78.75; Corporation Annual Report: $150

Georgia
LLC filing fees: $100; LLC Annual Report: $50; Incorporation filing fees: $100 Corporation Publication fees: $150 (required for Corps); Corporation Initial Report: $50; Corporation Annual Report: $50

Hawaii
LLC filing fees: $50; LLC Annual Report: $15; Incorporation filing fees: $50; Corporation Annual Report: $15

Idaho
LLC filing fees: $100; LLC Annual Report: $0; Incorporation filing fees: $101; Corporation Annual Report: $0

Illinois
LLC filing fees: $500; LLC Annual Report: $305; Incorporation filing fees: $175; Corporation Annual Report: $155

Indiana
LLC filing fees: $90; LLC Annual Report: $30; Incorporation filing fees: $90; Corporation Annual Report: $30

Iowa

LLC filing fees: $50; LLC Annual Report: $45; Incorporation filing fees: $50; Corporation Annual Report: $45

Kansas

LLC filing fees: $160; LLC Annual Report: $55; Incorporation filing fees: $90; Corporation Annual Report: $55

Kentucky

LLC filing fees: $55; LLC Annual Report: $15; Incorporation filing fees: $55; Corporation Annual Report: $15

Louisiana

LLC filing fees: $100; LLC Annual Report: $30; Incorporation filing fees: $100; Corporation Annual Report: $30

Maine

LLC filing fees: $175; LLC Annual Report: $85; Incorporation filing fees: $145; Corporation Annual Report: $85

Maryland

LLC filing fees: $155; LLC Annual Report: depends on revenue (min fee $300); Incorporation filing fees: $155; Corporation Annual Report: depends on revenue (min fee $300)

Massachusetts

LLC filing fees: $520; LLC Annual Report: $520; Incorporation filing fees: $295; Corporation Annual Report: $135

Michigan

LLC filing fees: $50; LLC Annual Report: $25; Incorporation filing fees: $60; Corporation Annual Report: $25

Minnesota

LLC filing fees: $160; LLC Annual Report: $0; Incorporation filing fees: $160; Corporation Annual Report: $0

Mississippi

LLC filing fees: $50; LLC Annual Report: $25; Incorporation filing fees: $50; Corporation Annual Report: $25

Missouri

LLC filing fees: $50; LLC Annual Report: $0; Incorporation filing fees: $58; Corporation Initial Report: $45; Corporation Annual Report: $45

Montana

LLC filing fees: $70; LLC Annual Report: $15; Incorporation filing fees: $70; Corporation Annual Report: $15

Nebraska

LLC filing fees: $120; LLC Publication fees: $150; LLC Annual Report: $26; Incorporation filing fees: $65; Corporation Publication fees: $150; Corporation Annual Report: $26

Nevada

LLC filing fees: $75; LLC Initial Report: $325; LLC Annual Report: $325; Incorporation filing fees: $75; Corporation Initial Report: $325; Corporation Annual Report: $325

New Hampshire

LLC filing fees: $100; LLC Annual Report: $100; Incorporation filing fees: $100; Corporation Annual Report: $100

New Jersey

LLC filing fees: $125; LLC Annual Report: $50; Incorporation filing fees: $125; Corporation Annual Report: $50

New Mexico

LLC filing fees: $50; LLC Annual Report: $0; Incorporation filing fees: $100; Corporation Initial Report: $25; Corporation Annual Report: $25

New York

LLC filing fees: $210; LLC Annual Report: $9; LLC Publication fees: Starting from $425-$1200; Incorporation filing fees: $145; Corporation Annual Report: $9

North Carolina

LLC filing fees: $125; LLC Annual Report: $202; Incorporation filing fees: $125; Corporation Annual Report: $20

North Dakota

LLC filing fees: $135; LLC Annual Report: $50; Incorporation filing fees: $100; Corporation Annual Report: $25

Ohio

LLC filing fees: $125; LLC Annual Report: $0; Incorporation filing fees: $125; Corporation Annual Report: $0

Oklahoma

LLC filing fees: $104; LLC Annual Report: $25; Incorporation filing fees: $52; Corporation Annual Report: $0

Oregon

LLC filing fees: $100; LLC Annual Report: $100; Incorporation filing fees: $100; Corporation Annual Report: $100

Pennsylvania

LLC filing fees: $125; LLC Annual Report: $0; Incorporation filing fees: $125; Corporation Annual Report: $0 Incorporation Publication fees: $299

Rhode Island

LLC filing fees: $150; LLC Annual Report: $50; Incorporation filing fees: $230; Corporation Annual Report: $50

South Carolina

LLC filing fees: $110; LLC Annual Report: $0; Incorporation filing fees: $135; Corporation Annual Report: $0; Incorporation Attorney Signature fees: $100

South Dakota

LLC filing fees: $150; LLC Annual Report: $50; Incorporation filing fees: $150; Corporation Annual Report: $50

Tennessee

LLC filing fees: $325; LLC Annual Report: $310; Incorporation filing fees: $125; Corporation Annual Report: $20

Texas

LLC filing fees: $310; LLC Annual Report: (depends on gross annual revenue); Incorporation filing fees: $310; Corporation Annual Report: (depends on gross annual revenue)

Utah

LLC filing fees: $72; LLC Annual Report: $15; Incorporation filing fees: $72; Corporation Annual Report: $15

Vermont

LLC filing fees: $125; LLC Annual Report: $25; Incorporation filing fees: $125; Corporation Annual Report: $35

Virginia

LLC filing fees: $104; LLC Annual Report: $50; Incorporation filing fees: $79; Corporation Annual Report: $100

Washington

LLC filing fees: $200; LLC Initial Report: $10; LLC Annual Report: $73; Incorporation filing fees: $200; Corporation Initial Report: $10; Corporation Annual Report: $73

West Virginia

LLC filing fees: $132; LLC Annual Report: $25; Incorporation filing fees: $82; Corporation Annual Report: $25

Wisconsin

LLC filing fees: $130; LLC Annual Report: $25; Incorporation filing fees: $100; Corporation Annual Report: $40

Wyoming

LLC filing fees: $103; LLC Annual Report: $52; Incorporation filing fees: $103; Corporation Annual Report: $52

Unified Carrier Registration (UCR)

The UCR fee for a maximum of two vehicles is $69. It increases to $206 when you have three to five vehicles.

3.9 Buying vehicles: New vs. Used

Choose a truck that is less than five years old and has a Detroit Diesel engine. The condition of the equipment acquired by you should be excellent. You can minimize your maintenance costs if you make a wise decision initially and pay a premium price on acquiring a truck for your trucking business. You may, however, purchase a used unit if you are sure about minimum future maintenance costs and have faith in the accuracy of its files.

A robust and roadworthy second-hand vehicle also benefits lower annual insurance premiums, making it a viable option for new businesses.

Although the above specifications will cost you more money, they will provide you with an average of eight to ten years of hassle-free operation. You can also avoid costly repairs. New truckers frequently make the mistake of cutting corners on equipment costs, only to come to regret their decision later in the future when the truck breaks down (numerous times) and requires constant repairs. A truck could indeed cost anywhere from $15,000 to $175,000. Moreover, it should not have covered a distance of more than 600,000 miles. It all depends on the vehicle you choose. You might be required to make an upfront payment in the range of $1,000 and $10,000.

Buying vs. Leasing

Owner-operators are in a unique position to make critical business decisions that will affect their long-term success. The semi-truck purchased by you can either be a source of financial gain or a source of financial loss, depending on your initial buying decisions. Concerning buying versus leasing decisions, it is all contingent on your specific circumstances and targets. The said will be the guiding factors in choosing between buying and leasing. Moreover, the truck type and your financial muscle shall also impact your decision about leasing and buying.

3.10 Buying a Semi-Truck as an Owner-operator

A new truck usually costs well over $100,000 on average. Are you in a position to commit this kind of investment to buy a truck? If not, look into financing options. In either case, you'll need to raise investment. You can also use the purchase for writing off tax obligations. You just have to hire the services of an accountant or tax professional before making the buying decision. You need to talk to the tax profession and get informed of all tax implications. You'll also save money on insurance because rates for used vehicles are comparatively lower than leased vehicles. Depending on the company issuing the loan, you may not be required to make a huge upfront payment if you have an excellent credit history. An extremely expensive truck could also result in an initial heavy down payment. You'll also get the most up-to-date mechanical technology with a new truck. New trucks are always more energy-efficient as compared to older models. Consequently, you would save money on operating costs and fuel.

If you want to buy a truck but the price tag of $100,000 or more is out of your price range, you could perhaps purchase a used truck for as little as $15,000. A used truck might save you from initial expense but it will cost you more in the long run due to repair and maintenance costs that would be required to keep it running. Furthermore, a factory warranty with a new truck will help you save money on service issues and any problems that arise during the warranty period.

3.11 Leasing a Semi-Truck as an Owner-operator

Leasing may be the best option if you can't afford to buy your truck or want to reduce your financial risks. The duration of a lease agreement could be of five years. Upon the lease agreement's expiry, you will have to return the truck. However, you then have the option to lease another truck for another period of five years. If you choose to quit the lease agreement before its expiry, you will be charged a penalty. The penalty amount is clearly defined in the lease agreement. Make sure you go through your lease agreement properly. There are frequent rules and requirements that you must follow while operating the truck. Your mileage may be restricted, similar to that of a personal vehicle.

3.12 Lease Types

You can choose from two lease types. These are conventional lease and lease-to-own. Both types do not require you to raise a huge amount of capital in the very beginning. It would help if you remembered that you will not always need good credit as this condition is relaxed in some of the leases. In a conventional lease, you have to make monthly payments for a fixed period. When your contract expires, you can hand over the truck to the lessor. Another advantage is learning about the real-world costs of owning a truck while avoiding some of the annoyances. Many conventional leases include a servicing agreement that covers any maintenance or service requirements that the vehicle may require during the lease term. When you sign a lease-to-own agreement, you have the option to buy the semi-truck at the expiry of the lease. The contract will include a buy-out price. You can negotiate this buy-out price before the signing of the lease agreement. You'll need to move adequate merchandise or goods to raise funds for the monthly payment of this type of lease. If you don't, your truck may be repossessed by the leasing company.

What is the best choice?

The two options are set apart by your decision to buy or lease a semi-truck. A conventional lease can usually be a short-term commitment. Moreover, it gives you the freedom to return the truck to the leasing company at the end of the contract. You'll have to spend less money up front, but you would not be able to build equity. Overall, you may end up paying more than if you had bought it outright. A leased semi-trucks insurance is usually on the higher side compared to a purchased semi-truck. You can't personalize it by modifying or updating it like you would if you owned it. Purchasing or leasing a semi-truck is, in the end, a financial decision. But it doesn't stop there; as an owner-operator, you must also consider your long-term goals and vision.

Reasons to lease trucks

When it comes to running a trucking business, possessing a company truck creates a valuable asset because it can transport equipment and perform other tasks. You should not be perplexed by the task of making a buying decision for the truck. You can lease a commercial truck instead of buying one, as most business owners do today. Here are some of the most significant advantages of leasing a company truck rather than purchasing a new one.

Leasing is convenient and yields more profits

One of the main advantages of leasing a commercial truck is that it does not necessitate a large upfront investment. Unlike buying a car, leasing has no hidden costs like taxes, towing, overhead, or other expenses. Truck owners must also cover finance charges and pay a sales tax, in addition to the large upfront costs. Because the monthly payments are lower when you lease a commercial truck, you can increase your profits for your company. As a result, you'll be able to keep sufficient funds in the bank account of your company. Furthermore, this also requires less paperwork, thus allowing you to concentrate on your business growth.

No Depreciation Costs

You will be unaffected if the value of your leased truck decreases due to depreciation. To put it another way, you won't have to worry about depreciation costs. These costs generally pose a problem when you buy a new truck. Leasing does not affect your company's net worth and does not appear on your CFO's balance sheet.

Less Maintenance and Repair Costs

Another advantage of leasing is that it helps you to reduce your maintenance and repair costs.

Repairs and maintenance costs, like oil changes, tires, and routine inspections, are covered under a full-service lease.

When you own a truck, you have to pay for repairs and maintenance costs.

Relieves you of issues linked with vehicle ownership

When you give up on owning a truck and opt for leasing a truck, you avoid the hassles that come with owning a vehicle.

For example, you won't be dealing with potential compliance issues, fees associated with driver replacement, or costs associated with driver training.

Another issue with owning a company truck is that drivers will leave for companies with more advanced equipment.

More flexibility

Many leasing companies do not demand an upfront payment. This freedom lends flexibility to leasing a truck as compared to purchasing one. You also have the liberty of returning your leased vehicle at the end of your lease period.

Furthermore, the terms of a lease include a fixed, consistent payment, which can free up capital and make your finances more flexible. This is especially useful when making business investments or paying for emergency business repairs.

24/7 emergency roadside breakdown assistance

Leasing provides you with the assurance that you will be rescued if your truck breaks down.

When you purchase a full-service lease, you can have your leasing company handle vehicle breakdowns instead of owning a truck.

When your truck breaks down, you can call a seasoned mechanic to help you with the truck repair. These professionals are equipped to handle flat tires, towing, and a variety of other issues.

Common leasing terms

It's important to have an in-depth knowledge of the basic leasing terms:

Depreciation

Depreciation is the amount that results in the value reduction of the truck during the lease period.

Residual

Residual value is the book value of a vehicle at the expiry of the lease.

Capitalized cost

This is also called "cap cost." This is the negotiated selling price of a vehicle. It does not include extra fees, like an acquisition fee. However, you may include these in your lease payments.

Money factor

This is the finance charge. It is usually expressed as a fraction.

Leasing vs. Renting

You must know that leasing a truck is not the same as renting one. There are, however, few similarities between leasing and renting, yet they're not the same.

- Time frame is one of the key differences. Truck rentals are to be paid for a couple of days or weeks. On the contrary, leasing a truck entails regular payments for a longer period.
- There is also a difference between the two parties which lease or rent a truck. Rental agencies usually rent vehicles at stores or airports. On the other hand, leased vehicles are leased by fleet leasing companies or auto dealerships.

- You cannot secure ownership of a rented vehicle. However, you can own a leased truck at the expiry of the lease. When you lease a truck, you are buying a truck for a specific period, and you have to make regular payments till the expiry of the lease.

Critical consideration

As the cost of new vehicles rises, leasing becomes a more attractive proposition. You have enhanced flexibility, minimal commitment, and no worries about depreciation, maintenance, or repairs when you lease a truck. Your business will be more profitable, and you will have more time to concentrate on it if you spend less money on leasing. Consider how you can exchange a leased commercial truck for a newer model with the latest technology. You can deduct business expenses incurred while driving your leased truck, just like vehicle owners. You can do this by using the standard mileage rate.

Getting insurance

One of the highest annual fixed costs is insurance coverage. Several factors determine the cumulative insurance costs. The age of your equipment, the commodities transported, and the location of your truck are some of the important factors that should be taken into consideration with the insurance coverage. When calculating your insurance premium, insurers take these factors into account. The annual insurance cost for your truck could be up to $10,000 per truck, based on its condition. This figure varies depending on the type of coverage, the vehicle's model, year and condition, and the driver's experience. You can install an FMCSA-registered electronic logging device to help you save money on insurance.

CDL license endorsements

You might need multiple endorsements for becoming capable of operating hazardous cargoes or specialized vehicles. These endorsements must be added to the CDL. Given below are some of the endorsements that you might require for the said purpose:

H — HAZMAT

This endorsement is required to transport hazardous materials and must be placarded under 49 CFR part 172, subpart F. A "hazardous" material, according to government regulations, could include explosives, gases, flammable liquids, and combustible liquids. It includes all those materials that are capable of causing any harm. You should be aware that this endorsement costs approximately $100. Moreover, it requires $87 for TSA screening.

P — Passenger transport vehicle operator

This endorsement permits you to drive more than 16 passengers. You have to pay $14, which is the average fee, for this endorsement.

It is also mandatory for the drivers to sit in a 20-question test. The drivers also need to pass a skill test.

X — Transporting HAZMAT in a tanker

This endorsement permits you to operate vehicles that carry waste or hazardous materials in placarded amounts. H & N endorsements are also required for the said purpose. You have to pay $14, which is the average fee, for this endorsement. It is also mandatory for the drivers to sit in a 30-question tanker test. It is also mandatory for the drivers to sit in a 20-question hazmat test.

Conclusion

You should set aside a minimum of five thousand dollars for marketing and customer acquisition in addition to the expenses listed above. This could include creating a website, establishing a social media presence, generating advertisements, and printing business cards. Consider purchasing a compliant and ELD solution to help reduce some variable costs, such as reducing fuel waste by reducing idling, enhancing driver safety and limiting potential liabilities by tracking driver behavior, and slashing administrative costs through automation like IFTA reporting and vehicle maintenance.

The role of owner-operator

An owner-operator truck driver is usually an independent driver. His job is to transport goods and carry freight. As an owner-operator, you have your vehicle, and you operate it yourself rather than working for a trucking company. It is your discretion to decide about the performance and allocation of tasks. You have to determine routes, load and unload your truck, and deliver items according to the terms of your contract. Some jobs are no-touch freight, meaning you only move from one point to another point, and you get to choose which tasks you do as the owner. Owner-operator truck drivers must also deal with tire and engine issues, as well as maintain their vehicles.

What is an owner-operator?

An owner-operator is the main stakeholder in a company. This position entails overseeing all operations from beginning to end, including the hiring of drivers and staff. In addition to those mentioned above, it is the key responsibility of an owner-operator to devise a marketing strategy for the successful running of the business. Once new employees have been hired, an owner-operator is responsible for ensuring that they perform effectively and efficiently under its objectives. Although owner-operators are not required to have a specific educational background, their knowledge and experience in business will greatly impact the company's success. You will have to work for longer periods because of your role as the main stakeholder of the business. You will have to travel frequently to meet with suppliers and contractors. You should be an expert in customer service and must possess excellent interpersonal skills and strong business acumen if you want to be successful as an owner-operator.

The top responsibilities of an owner-operator

Every day, owner-operators face the challenge of being credible drivers as well as professional business owners. Owning a business and managing the associated responsibilities could be overwhelming for new owner-operators. It is not a new concept to be a responsible driver. Safety laws and regulations are constantly changing, so even the most experienced owner-operator must stay current. Here are some helpful hints for staying safe and profitable on the road:

Pre-Trip inspections

You should make it a habit to undertake pre-trip inspections. This will help you in identifying and fixing any technical problems. Your job is to ensure the safety of your rig and the safety of others on the road.

Logbook

It's important to maintain an updated status of your logbooks. DOT has made it mandatory to maintain a logbook of your driving since the receipts and toll fees will be used to vet your logbook, so you have to keep it as accurate as possible. You also have to remain compliant.

Practice safe driving habits

Safe driving habits are critical to the success of your business and the hassle-free operations of your truck. It would help if you did not drive in unsafe driving conditions. It's especially important to get enough sleep so you can drive safely.

Choose loads wisely

Making wise decisions about the selection of loads is an important factor in the trucking business. Nobody knows your schedule and your ability better than you. You must not take loads that you cannot carry and handle. You should never compromise your reputation and safety in search of profits.

CSA Compliance

You have to make sure that both you and your rig comply with all the rules and regulations –federal, state, county, and city. Failure to comply with the CSA safety standards can result in shutting down your business revoking your license.

Personal health

Your health is more important than anything else. A healthy person can work as well as perform better in the competitive trucking industry. The CSA has a list of physical requirements that must be met to be considered a fit driver. For your business, you would need to lift and carry items regularly. An illness or injury could also keep you from working for a while. As a result, maintaining a healthy and injury-free lifestyle is critical to your long-term success. It is critical to be well-organized and financially responsible for achieving success. This can be a substantial shift for company drivers who previously did not have to shoulder the following additional responsibilities:

Calculate your profit potential

Any business owner's top priorities are to generate maximum profits and operate at the lowest possible cost. Keep yourself up to date on your company's performance.

Communicate effectively

It is your key responsibility to keep your customers updated about your schedule. You must never fail to inform your customers of any changes. You should not hesitate in informing your customers about any change in schedule due to mechanical problems, inclement weather, or any other reason.

Be on time

You should have an impeccable record of picking up and delivering. These are the most significant factors for your customers. It is you who can make or break the business with your style and attitude.

Control costs

Monitoring of fuel usage facilitates an owner-operator in getting the desired mileage. You must check your equipment and do regular maintenance and repairs periodically. This way, you can avert major mechanical breakdowns and expenses in the future.

Pay your taxes

When you were a company driver, it was your carrier who was responsible for paying your taxes. As an owner-operator, you have to determine the precise amount and send it to the IRS quarterly. You can maximize your tax returns by keeping accurate records of estimated tax payments.

You must be able to keep accurate financial records and set money aside for taxes. This practice will help you in alleviating stress.

Be productive

You should always keep track of the freight schedule and make arrangements accordingly. You don't have to take time off just because you can. So, when planning your vacation days, make sure you consider your company's goals.

To understand how to manage your time and schedule best, you need to know the breakeven miles.

The minimum number of miles you must run each month to offset the expenses is your breakeven mileage.

Your profitability starts after covering your expenses. You're responsible for a lot more than just driving a truck down the highway.

The role of a driver is complex and difficult and, at times, intimidating because it entails so many responsibilities.

However, once you've mastered the art of handling multiple tasks and responsibilities, you will start enjoying working as an owner-operator.

Owner-operator responsibilities

Listed below are the responsibilities of the owner-operator:

- Hauling cargo from one point to another point in compliance with the instructions of company dispatchers.
- You have to plan travel routes strategically, ensuring the timely delivery of all loads.
- You should always review dispatchers' instructions before deliveries. This will minimize as well as protect you from any errors or miscommunications.
- You should perform inspections of the designated truck before and after each delivery. This way, you can safeguard against any mechanical breakdown.

- You should instantly inform the management about any mechanical issues that might prevent the truck from hauling the load.
- You must maintain a logbook with an accurate account of the number of hours worked, rest periods, and mileage covered.
- You should always submit cargo documents to customers. You should also take their signatures to confirm receipt of the correct cargo.
- You must never forget to notify dispatch of any damaged cargo.
- You should always supervise the safe loading and unloading of cargo.

Owner-operator requirements

Listed below are the requirements for becoming an owner-operator:

- High school diploma or GED.
- Completion of a tractor-trailer driver training program is beneficial.
- Valid commercial driver's license (CDL).
- A clean driving record.
- Proven truck driving experience.
- In-depth knowledge of road safety regulations
- In-depth knowledge of loading and unloading procedures, as well as weight restrictions.

- You must be able to utilize GPS systems, road maps, and routing software.
- You should have no problems concentrating on customers.
- You must possess time management, organizational, and problem-solving skills.
- Effective communication skills.

3.13 Difference between an owner operator truck driver and a company truck driver

The driving skills and requirements for an owner-operator and a company truck driver are the same. An important distinction is that an owner-operator carries some financial risk like any other business owner.

As an owner-operator, you receive full payment and are responsible for allocating necessary funds to upkeep your vehicle and tools.

This arrangement is often more lucrative than contracting through an agency or working for a trucking company, but it comes with greater risk and responsibility; repairs, time off, and other unforeseen expenses can reduce your profits.

3.14 Benefits of owner operator trucking business

The trucking industry is booming and is in high demand, thanks to the expanding economy and the growing popularity of online shopping.

You can be independent

Many people who begin a trucking business have previously worked in the shipping industry, either as shippers or carriers. As an owner-operator, you have schedule flexibility, which allows you to achieve a better work-life balance. You also have more control over business decisions as compared to many other people in the industry.

You can spend more time with your families

You set your working hours as an owner-operator, which means you can spend more time teaching junior how to catch a football, have weekly date nights with the significant other, or even go on real sightseeing trips.

As an owner-operator, you earn more

This position is for a self-motivated self-starter who isn't looking for a steady paycheck or a 9-5 schedule. Because your earning is determined by your output, you will make as much money as you want as long as you are willing to put in the effort.

You do not have to commute much

One of the best things about being an owner-operator is that you can do almost all of your work from the comfort of your own home. Because much of TMS is web-based, you can use your PC or laptop to access all load boards. Aside from that, all you need is a cell phone to take calls, and you're good to go. Working from the comfort of your own home is the ultimate dream of those who work for a living.

You do not need to commit heavy investment to initiate the business

If you have good credit, you should be able to start your owner-operator business for less than $20,500. It's your choice because you're the boss. In most start-up scenarios, there are significant upfront associated costs with starting a business. Insurance, licenses, software, office space, and payroll are all expenses. Working with an established freight broker as a freight agent can help you avoid these high costs.

Your schedule is flexible

If, as an owner-operator, you want to take a break, you have the option of doing so. You can hire dispatchers to ensure that connections with shippers are maintained during their absence. They can move the loads from the customers while you're away from the office.

An owner-operator has defined overheads

If you run a one-person show and work from home, you'll often find that you're able to save money on overhead. You'll spend the majority of your time on the phone, negotiating with shippers and carriers, as well as researching and tracking shipments. The overhead to run your business is relatively low for most owner-operators, especially when compared to other businesses and the number of expenses they must rack up every month. In reality, an independent agent only has to pay for a few necessary expenses. Unless you want to open an office in a building, the position does not demand much to get started.

There are no territory restrictions

Trucking business services can be provided across the country or even around the world in some cases. Domestic shipping is a much easier operation, and owner-operators use it more frequently. In essence, there are no limitations to how big your company can grow. This presents fantastic opportunities for those looking to make a name for themselves in business and scale their brand to its full potential.

Education is not a prerequisite

Being an owner-operator is one of the career paths which defines the conventional wisdom that obtaining a college diploma or "education" is the only way to achieve true financial security and success. Success in the logistics industry is simple, but it's not easy. It all begins at the bottom, just like any other career or job. Starting in the industry is a great way to learn the ropes. It's time to start forming long-term business relationships once you've gained industry knowledge and can speak the language. Along the way, the educational process is incorporated. Working from home and earning $150,000+ per year isn't a big problem. It simply takes hard work and patience to establish a reputation in the industry.

You can earn as much as you desire

This is a thriving industry, and your only limit to earning potential is your devotion to success. There's plenty of work to go around, particularly now that e-commerce is on the rise. Shippers are increasingly sending goods from warehouses and distribution centers, which can only mean one thing for you: more earning opportunities.

You can go for unlimited growth

The more your trucking business expands, the more you improve your industry knowledge. And the more you advance in the leadership, the more you'll meet new industry contacts in cities all over the country, from Seattle to Yonkers. As an owner-operator, your world is expanding exponentially, and so is your income.

It enables you to initiate a stable family business

Once you've made it as an owner-operator, there's only one way to go: up—including building a thriving business in which the rest of the family can participate. Your children can begin learning the ropes, you can hire people you trust, and your company can grow to be one of the most valuable in your state. The options are limitless.

Owner operator trucking business is lucrative for the family

A profitable family-run trucking business company is a valuable asset that can provide for your family for generations, whether you keep it running or sell it for a profit. It's a win for all parties involved. You have a bright future ahead of you. Working for oneself provides a unique sense of meaning and value. Your successes, as well as your failures, are completely transparent. Each one contributes to making you a better person than the day before. You will be remembered as a leader by your friends, family, and associates, and you'll have a positive impact on their lives.

You can keep the business in the family

The trucking business is a very valuable gift that can be passed down for generations. It's an opportunity to put not only yourself but your entire family in a position to succeed. A trucking company business is a working asset that can add value in various ways, including by creating jobs, giving back to the community, and providing a valuable service that helps other businesses grow. Your loved ones will be grateful for all of your efforts and sacrifices in providing them with such a wide range of opportunities.

CHAPTER 4:

Trucking Business Types

The uses of road transportation, like light trucks and semi-trailers, is referred to as the trucking industry to move your goods across overland routes. The most common use is to transport goods from manufacturing plants to retail distribution centers. However, there are other common uses in the construction industry, such as building materials and waste. Trucking accounts for most overland freight movement in the United States, with a market worth $791.7 billion in 2019. There were over 947,000 truck drivers employed in the United States at the time, which was less than the industry requires. In general, the trucking industry in the United States can be separated into the following types:

4.1 Full truckload carriers

Full truckload carriers are a type of trucking company that makes money by transporting freight for other companies. Working for a full truckload carrier means you're employed by a company that doesn't manufacture or produce anything. Instead, full truckload carriers sell their fleet capacity to other businesses that require logistical assistance and supply chain management. Full truckload carriers typically contract out their trucks, trailers, and drivers to another company needing their services. Because these businesses do not manufacture or ship their goods, their entire business model is based on other businesses' freight demands. FTL carriers transport large quantities of homogeneous cargo, usually enough to fill a semi-trailer or container. Fleets in the FTL sector can be privately owned, such as by a large manufacturer who wants to distribute their products or rented.

In most cases, for-hire carriers provide additional logistics and transportation services, like intermodal transportation options. Old Dominion was the largest US FTL carrier by market value in 2019, with over four billion dollars in total operating revenue across all operating segments. J.B. Hunt and Knight-Swift are two other well-known FTL carriers, with revenue of over $9.1 billion and 4.7 billion dollars, respectively, in 2019. Working for this type of trucking company has its drawbacks, as freight contracts change hands and are offered to other trucking companies to bid on. You may currently work for one of these companies and enjoy hauling freight for them, but that does not guarantee that they'll always win the bid for that customer's freight contract. This implies that you should be aware of the possibility of the freight changing. Full truckload companies frequently have multiple customers to protect themselves from the loss of one customer's freight. Another disadvantage of working for a truckload carrier is that drivers are usually part of a larger over-the-road network. This isn't always the case, but a full truckload carrier's driver fleet will typically include a large percentage of OTR drivers, and as a new driver in the industry, this may be where you'll have to start if you want to advance.

4.2 Private Fleets

There are hundreds of businesses that manufacture a product and manage its distribution and supply chain. Private fleets are companies that provide their trucks, trailers, drivers, and the actual freight being transported. Private fleet truck drivers are usually employees of the company that owns the freight. Frito Lay, for example, is a private fleet. Frito-Lays manufacture the product and have their delivery drivers who work within their supply chain. FedEx and UPS also own private fleets. They have their fleet of truck drivers who work for them, but it's not uncommon for a private fleet to require assistance with freight capacity. FedEx and UPS, for example, may not have enough trucks and drivers to meet all of their freight demands, in which case they may be forced to broker their excess freight to other full truckload carriers. Drivers who work for private fleets are typically paid more and have more experience. Getting hired on by a private fleet is usually more difficult. Working for a private fleet has the disadvantage that your job security is determined by a single company's overall financial health. As a result, you are essentially putting all of your eggs in one basket as a driver. Because drivers who work for private fleets haul the same product, if the company struggles or things slow down, their miles may suffer due to their lack of freight to haul.

4.3 Less-than-truckload carriers

On the other hand, LTL carriers transport larger shipments than parcels but are not large enough to fill a trailer. To save time and money, many LTL carriers would therefore transport multiple shipments at the same time. FedEx Freight is the largest LTL carrier, with over 7.4 billion dollars in revenue from LTL shipments in 2019. The next largest carriers after FedEx are Old Dominion, XPO Logistics, and YRC Freight, which generated between three and four billion dollars in revenue from LTL shipments in that year. There is a sizable segment of the trucking industry that specializes in less than truckload freight. This is also known as LTL. When it comes to shipping products from point A to point B, many products are being shipped to and from consumers, but less than truckload carriers come into play when a product is too large to be sent through the regular postal service. A less-than-truckload carrier will typically use a 53' trailer or doubles to transport smaller items that need to be delivered to homes or businesses across the United States. One less-than-truckload trailer could be transporting tens of thousands of different products to a variety of customers. LTL companies will have their drivers and dispatch schedule the delivery of these goods to the customer's residence, or they may have the customer pick up the freight from a local distribution center. Companies that specialize in LTL transport usually employ two different types of drivers. The first driver is a line hauler, who transports dedicated freight from one location to another. This could be from one distribution center to another. Because these drivers commute, they usually get consistent mileage and home time regularly.

The second type of driver employed by LTL companies is a city driver who operates a day cab and makes local deliveries. These drivers are usually home every day, but they must navigate city traffic and meet with many customers. A city LTL driver handles a lot of freight because one load may have 12 or more stops.

4.4 Couriers

Carriers of non-palletized as well as light goods, such as parcels, make up the courier sector. The US Postal Service, FedEx, and UPS are the three major players in this industry in the United States. Package delivery revenues appear to be higher than FLT and LTL: FedEx Express reported just over 27.6 billion US dollars in revenue for their 2020 fiscal year, while UPS reported approximately 46.5 billion US dollars in domestic package delivery revenue in 2019. However, not all of this revenue can be traced back to the trucking industry's courier sector.

4.5 Backhaul

Backhauling (also known as "backloading") is the process of planning roundtrip hauls and mapping out routes to ensure that goods are transported on each leg of a truck's journey. Increased vehicle as well as driver utilization enhances efficiency and eliminates unnecessary trips, reducing fuel consumption. Backhauling improves fleet operations. As a fleet owner, the last thing you want is for your trucks to be idle, burning expensive fuel while only transporting your drivers on the roads when they could be transporting more cargo. That's why backhauling, a practice in which a truck picks up an additional load after a haul is completed and transports it back to a location near or at the truck's original starting point, is a good idea. Internal backhauling is the process of transporting a company's goods or products back to their original location. External backhauling, or transporting third-party freight to and from the original delivery point, is done by most fleets. It entails regular communication with other carriers known to operate in the same "lanes," as well as brokers who schedule with other carriers to plan the movement of goods before dispatching and delivery. Backhauling in the moving industry refers to multiple customers sharing space in a moving truck for a discounted price. While some moving companies arrange round-trips to minimize empty vehicles, backhauling in the moving industry particularly refers to multiple customers sharing space in a moving truck for a discounted price.

It only makes sense if the customers are moving to the same area and don't have much furniture to transport, but it's a common industry strategy that allows moving companies to provide more effective service to the customers while saving fuel and maximizing employee utilization.

4.6 Household Movers

Drivers who work for household moving companies have to combine physical labor with freight transportation. Most household movers' work is from single customers who need their belongings moved due to a relocation need. Working for a household moving company may appeal to people who enjoy physical labor or want to stay in shape. Each company offers different relocation packages, so some may offer moving packages that include the driver packing the customers' belongings with the help of some local help. The driver may be required to pack the customers' goods, load them into the trailer, drive the freight from point A to point B, and then offload the household items at the customers' new location, depending on the company. The disadvantage of this type of work is that it increases the risk of injury due to the physical labor involved.

4.7 Inter-modal

Tractor-trailer transportation isn't the only way that freight is transported around the world. Local drivers who transport rail containers to and from the rail yard are known as inter-modal drivers. Rail freight shipping can be a much more cost-effective option for many businesses. The problem with shipping freight by rail is that shippers must still deliver their goods to the rail depot and ensure that the freight is picked up and delivered to the final customer. This distribution process necessitates the use of more hands to handle the freight. To get the freight to the rail yard, you'll need one truck and one driver. The freight is then transported by rail for the majority of the journey. Once the freight arrives at the final destination, it must be picked up by another truck and driver to be delivered to the final customer. The normal truckload process would have required only one driver and one truck to transport the freight from point A to point B, but because the freight was shipped by rail, the shipping process required two drivers and two trucks to complete. Because shipping freight by rail requires more hands, it typically provides good jobs for drivers who want to haul freight locally. You may want to check into intermodal freight transport firms if you reside near a shipping port or major rail hub.

4.8 Flatbed trucking service

The best trucks to load and unload cargo quickly and easily are flatbed trucks. This truck is excellent for transporting goods that have already been organized into shipping containers, vehicles, or other weather-resistant materials. Industries like construction and farming commonly use flatbed trucking services to transport oversized machinery and building supplies.

4.9 Refrigerated trucks or reefer trucks

Food-related shipments are usually temperature-controlled shipments. When a product requires a specific temperature to preserve its quality and taste, it will be loaded into a truck with the necessary equipment to keep the temperature consistent. Perishable goods require temperature-controlled trucking services. Produce, meats, cheeses, fish, and poultry can all be shipped using these trucks. Temperature-controlled trucks are also used by the pharmaceutical, medical, and chemical industries to transport perishable cargo. These unique trucks can help you control a wide range of conditions, including temperature and humidity. They also offer FTL and LTL options and special monitoring services that save you from any depression. A backup system is usually in place. If one of the cooling systems fails, another will kick in to keep the items from spoiling.

This is a service frequently used by farmers and food manufacturers, such as making ice cream or meat that must remain frozen. There are particularly unique trucks for various refrigeration requirements, plus several trucking companies that provide these services to their customers.

4.10 Expedited trucking service

This is also called Straight Truck Delivery Service. This method is used to move cargo from Point A to Point B quickly anywhere and anytime. This method is used where cargo is too large or too fragile to be transported by air.

4.11 White glove service

This specialized service is designed for transporting fragile items. This service is also used when you require and prefer the services of a professional team to pack and unpack your belongings for you. Unlike standard freight services, White glove services usually arrive at a designated location, pack and load the items for you. They will transport the items to the destination by truck. There they will unpack the items and remove all packing materials from your location. It's a complete package.

4.12 Door-to-Door

These services can easily be witnessed across the country. These services usually take place at the point of origin or the manufacturer.

When you purchase an item online or through a catalog, the delivery of that item is ensured by a trucking company that picks up the product from its location and delivers it to the customer. Usually, the goods are picked up from a warehouse. The goods are then transported to a port.

They are shipped and delivered to the consumer by another entity.

4.13 Business to Business

The same principles apply to business-to-business transportation as they do to door-to-door transportation. However, shipment sizes are typically much larger, as is the truck used to transport the shipment. While smaller trucks can be used for door-to-door delivery in several cases, tractor-trailers are frequently used to transport bulk goods from one location to another. The following are a few of the commodities that are transported in this manner:

- Furniture
- Dried foods that do not need to be refrigerated
- Manufactured items
- Electronics
- Industrial parts
- Industrial supplies

4.14 Heavy Haul or Specialized

Government agencies and businesses frequently use heavy haul or specialized services. The items transported by specialized services are either too big to fit on a regular truck or extremely heavy to meet the maximum load capacity of a regular truck. The transported items are usually very expensive, and they can include:

- Boats
- Planes
- Modular homes
- Generators
- Transformers

A score of heavy haul items is shipped every day. These items usually consume too much time for shipping purposes because of their weight and size. Therefore, they required appropriate time for shipment of time-sensitive items.

4.15 Tanker

Tankers are usually used for hauling liquids. Liquids could include gasoline, milk, etc. People hired to haul tankers are specially trained as they have the ability and skills to manage the constantly changing center of gravity.

4.16 Bull Hauler

Bull haulers pull trailers are specially designed trailers. These are used to transport live animals. Bull haulers need to be aware of various regulations and rules that must be complied with while hauling live animals.

4.17 Auto Hauler

Auto haulers are specialized trailers. These are designed to haul all types of vehicles. Auto haulers need to be aware of various regulations and rules that must be complied with while hauling vehicles. Therefore, they have to be more responsible and specially trained for carrying out the said task.

4.18 Container Hauler

Container haulers transport Container haulers usually transport metal containers. These are generally used for imported goods. A driver usually picks up the container from ports or terminals. Then he distributes the picked-up container to other ports or terminals.

4.19 Hopper (or Grain Hauler)

It is a specially designed trailer. It is used for dumping its contents. Bulk loads, like grain and corn, are usually transported by these specially designed trailers.

CHAPTER 5:

Marketing Strategy for Owner Operator Trucking Business

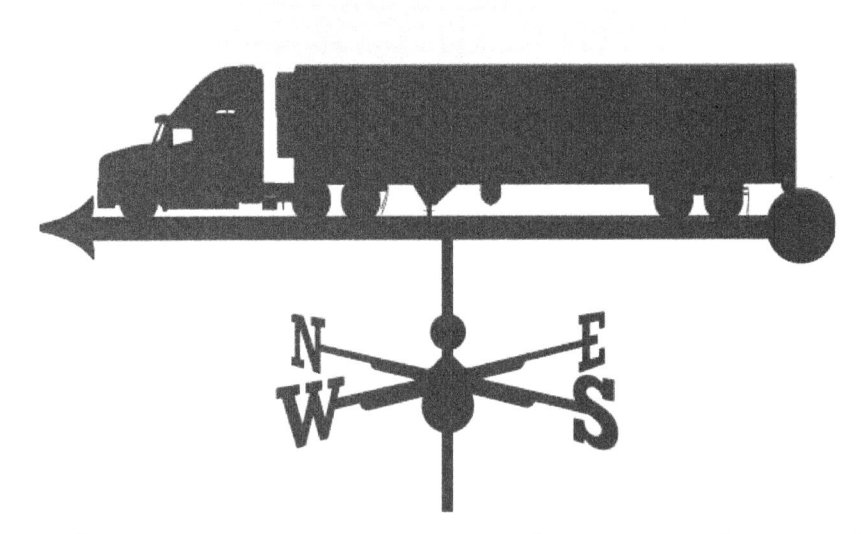

As an owner-operator, you have to employ sound and tested trucking business principles, as many of the industry's most successful owners have done for decades. Moreover, you need to formulate an effective marketing strategy to create your business niche, brand image and penetrate the market using social media. You also need to develop a website for creating awareness and reaching out to customers. We have discussed every aspect below to help you promote and profitably run your business.

5.1 Learn to distinguish yourself from the competition

The trucking industry is fiercely competitive, as well as shippers have a plethora of options for getting their goods to market. You must stand out from the crowd if you want to attract business. It is the responsibility of the business owner to create a customer experience that is so compelling that their business is assured. Trucking companies should differentiate between coffee and water if they can differentiate between coffee and water. Customers will look at the price if they don't notice a difference. Surprisingly, 60% to 70% of people in most businesses cannot explain why you are a better option than your competitors. Three factors hamper differentiation:

- Instead of focusing on what your competitors are doing, concentrate on what your customers want.
- Because of the Internet, which has dramatically changed the sales process "from delivering information to providing wisdom," competition has gotten tougher.

- Complacency breeds familiarity. Customers who have been with you for a long time should not be taken for granted.

Clarity, creativity, communication, and a customer-focused experience are the four cornerstones of differentiation.

Clarity

You must be clear about your advantages and what makes you stand out to differentiate yourself. You should be aware of who you are as well as who you are not. Emotion takes precedence over economics, and mindshare takes precedence over market share. To create clarity, you must develop a high concept, a short and strong statement about who you are and how you are different or better. It should pique the listener's interest in learning more about you. Furthermore, the statement must be brief and concise because you only have seven seconds to capture someone's attention. You must use your high concept repeatedly and integrate it into everything you do once you have developed it.

Creativity

It's the next pillar, but the good news is that you only need to change one aspect of your business to achieve it. You must first create that one thing before aggressively marketing it.

Communication

People nowadays are looking for more than just a list of facts and figures.

People's learning styles have evolved as well. You must alter the communication style so that you can engage customers through compelling stories.

This can be accomplished by telling a story about how one of your customer's businesses improved due to something you did for him.

Eyes on the customer

The final pillar is to put the customer first. Do you have any idea how it feels to do business with you? You should conduct a self-audit of your own customer experience. Owners and managers are focused on transactions, but the experiences keep customers coming back and generate referral business. T

The best way to audit your company is to imagine what would happen if everything went perfectly for the customer. Determine what that would entail, and then outline the steps you'll need to take to get there, as well as the obstacles you'll need to overcome. Your goal is to provide the best possible customer experience to every customer and prospect.

5.2 Manage the transportation costs effectively

Transportation costs and efficiencies have a significant impact on a trucking business, and this is one of the areas in which a trucking business's profitability can be lost if not managed properly. But it's not all about rates and prices. Organic ways for an owner-operator to maintain/increase profitability include new business, client retention, development, and growth.

5.3 Be reliable if you want to grow

One of the most important attributes a client looks for in a trucking company is reliability and market presence. In your dealings with customers, be dependable, punctual, transparent, and honest.

5.4 Use smart tactics

Warehouses, carriers, truckers, depots, clearing agents, pack houses, and other service providers are all used by a trucking company. It is critical for you as an owner-operator to get a dedicated procurement person and team in charge of procuring various services, as finding the ideal service to cost ratio can be difficult, and your quotes may become uncompetitive as a result. The availability of an effective, efficient process allows you to benchmark and find the proper mix of cost, service coverage, and reputation required to handle your customer's business effectively.

5.5 Optimize the processes

The trucking company business is a delicate, labor-intensive, and process-intensive business because it must cover activities by road. Any processes that are not observed appropriately or completed on time can result in additional costs that eat into the company's profits.

In specialized businesses such as project cargo and perishable cargoes, these additional costs have the power to wipe out the company's overall profits.

As a result, it's critical that operational processes for the different kinds of shipments handled and the various modes of transportation are properly mapped and recorded.

Digitalization has recently played a significant role in assisting business owners in optimizing their processes and those of their customers, to the point where it has created a new generation of digital companies for whom process optimization has become a USP.

5.6 Control overheads

Overheads are disastrous for the bottom line in any business, and if they aren't controlled, they can quickly spiral out of control. This is particularly true for owner-operators who own and operate their trucks. Lean businesses not only save money on trucking business operations, but they also have the flexibility to provide better service without making substantial or additional capital investments. In a market where providers must compete by differentiating their service offerings, the owner-operator can give consumers a powerful value proposition by lowering overheads and running a lean operation.

5.7 Avoid mistakes

It is really difficult for a trucking business owner to guarantee that their operation is error-free. The skill to avoid and recover from mistakes made in the business, on the other hand, is critical to a profitable trucking company operation. An effective way for an owner-operator to avoid costly mistakes is to use tried-and-true processes and hire the right people with the requisite experience and industry knowledge.

5.8 Create an organizational structure

Many companies' success depends on creating a clearly defined organizational structure, and everyone from management to the driver must understand and identify with the company's values, culture, strengths, mission, and vision for everyone to move in the same direction. The entire staff of the trucking company must be aware of the essence of the trucking company business.

5.9 Work on value addition

The trucking company operators can significantly increase their profitability by providing value-added services tailored to their customer's needs rather than providing the same service mix to all customers. At the best of times, global trade and logistics business can be complex, and catering to complex customer demands provides a freight forwarder with several opportunities to enhance their business prospects and build a positive reputation.

5.10 Know about the customer's business

Having a realistic understanding of the customer's business by asking the right questions and practical learning such as visiting the customer's business or factory to learn how things are done there, comprehending the organizational abilities, and so on, is a huge advantage for any owner-operator. Companies that understand their customers' businesses can better adapt to their customers' logistics needs, potentially saving both the company and the customer money.

5.11 Establish business relationships

In any business, having the right relationship works wonders, and by designating specialized as well as experienced staff within the organization in managing customers with special requirements, you could even manage any complex customer requirements, ensuring that they stick with your company and giving you with a viable volume and profitable revenue stream.

5.12 Work for efficient data management

Effective data management is one of the most important aspects of a trucking company's profitability. A trucking company handles a lot of data in any shipping transaction. A trucking company could collect and analyze a huge volume of real and tangible data by aggregating data flows, shaping them, and effectively using them.

This will help them understand their client's expectations and commodity movements, and cost implications.

5.13 Make a customer mix

Any trucking company needs to provide a good customer blend across various trade lanes and cargo types rather than operating with the same customer mix.

5.14 Be part of a Network

Being a part of a global freight network has several advantages for a trucking company, including:

- dependable partners who can assist with the customer's needs in a new country; and
- lower costs for the trucking company through volume-based rebates on rates at both origin and destination

5.15 Be proactive

Problems arise in all areas of business. It is up to the trucking company as the person in charge of handling the client's needs, being proactive, considering possible scenarios, and being ready for them when they appear.

5.16 Develop reputation

Suppose you truly care about your customers, their businesses, and their interests. In that case, you will gain a strong competitive advantage mostly as a trusted trucking company, leading to more repeat business and referrals.

5.17 Learn to control cost

In a trucking company business, cost control is critical, and failing to do so will have an immediate and negative impact on profits. Employee behavior is an important component of a good cost control system because employees are crucial in achieving an organization's goals, particularly cost control and reduction. Staff needs to be professionally trained and motivated to recognize the different cost levers and pressure points that can cause the company's and client's costs to rise. Experienced employees can bring tricks and tips to help businesses save money for themselves and their customers. Cost control measures should be in place and strategically controlled across all departments, especially those that deal with external service providers and external forces because their absence will significantly impact its profits.

5.18 Prepare for the future

Understandably, this is your primary focus if you're just getting started, but you must also consider the future. Create a succession plan that you can revisit and revise on an annual basis. Know how leadership will be passed on if it is required, whether through voluntary and involuntary departures.

5.19 Don't waste time inventing new ideas

Look for good ideas and products that are already being used by others that you really can integrate into your business. You don't have to do everything yourself; obtain ideas from other brokers, carriers, shippers, and even completely unrelated businesses. When freight broker Ron Williamson of Bloomingdale, Illinois, hired somebody to create a proprietary computer system, he learned the hard way. It was a mistake because it wasn't a fully integrated system that would save them time and increase productivity. Later on, they discovered a pre-packaged program that included all of the features they required.

5.20 Get rid of old trucks

Almost any trucking company will also have a service problem now and then, but if the problems become too frequent, you should eliminate the truck creating issues. If you're constantly having problems with your truck, you won't be able to keep your customers for very long. You must draw a line well before problems impact your own business.

5.21 Maintain a broad and diverse customer base

You'll need enough customers that losing one—or even a few—will not be disastrous. Allowing one customer to manipulate too much of your company's revenue is one of the worst mistakes people make. You'll be left with no customer if that customer pulls away without warning.

5.22 Get in the spotlight

Since this trucking industry is so heavily reliant on relationships and reputation, it's beneficial to keep yourself in the public eye as much as possible.

5.23 Be open to evolution

Though a trucking company can be very profitable on its own, it can also contribute to the development of many other transportation-related businesses, such as consulting and being a carrier. For example, Bill Tucker, a freight broker in Cherry Hill, New Jersey, provides a broad array of logistics services.

5.24 Get industry experience as well as research

Naturally, your communication and people skills will be crucial, as much of the work will be done over the phone or via email. Your skills would help you in negotiating and closing deals. Suppose you have – or can gain – significant experience in the transportation industry in another capacity. In that case, it will be very beneficial to your broker because you will be better connected with the industry's key players.

5.25 Protect your reputation

Concentrate on establishing the best possible reputation. When a shortcut appears but is a little shady, dare to pass it up, no matter how appealing the opportunity may appear. Many people in this industry require good, solid, honest, and reputable service, and that's where big money is in the long run. You survive, and you won't have many doors shut in your face because of a bad story that got out. A small village could be compared to the industry. Everyone is aware of each other's activities. It's amazing how quickly information spreads. Nothing should put you out of business and limit your success faster than a single bad transaction or a nasty court loss as a result of bad practices becoming public. You'll have to work up a sweat, tighten your belt from time to time, and persevere through some difficult times. But if you do things the right way every time, don't cut corners, provide excellent service, and maintain your integrity, you'll always have customers desirous of paying a fair price as well as good carriers eager to work with you.

5.26 Set prices

Determine a rate that is appropriate for each load.

5.27 Use advertising and marketing techniques that work

Keep track of your marketing efforts so that you can focus on the strategies that work while avoiding the ones that don't. Pens, note pads, caps, and T-shirts are good small giveaway items. Personal, as well as industry information in company newsletters, also receive a positive response. Donations to fundraising events may be beneficial (depending on the event and how well it is publicized. It's also a good idea to create a three-panel printed brochure that you can easily attach to letters, invoices, and checks. You can increase your brand recognition by placing ads in association newsletters, annual association, and industry directories regularly.

5.28 Set your goals and objectives

For your trucking company to be successful in a multichannel operation, you must achieve four main goals:
- Increased efficiency
- Increased sales
- Improved relationships
- Improved customer service

Each of these goals contains specific objectives that must be met within a given operation. Fortunately, there are tried-and-true best practices that can assist you in achieving your goals.

- The firm will design and build a transportation system to improve and protect the region's natural environment, historic and cultural resources, and communities.

- Improve inter-jurisdictional transportation and land-use planning coordination
- Obtain a more robust funding mechanism(s) for local and regional transportation system priorities, which cannot be realized with current and projected federal, state, and local funding.
- Options for international and inter-regional travel and commerce are to be encouraged.
- Provide a multimodal transportation system that is safe, efficient, and sustainable, with mobility and accessibility for all freight users.
- As it relates to the movement of goods, create an environment that promotes equitable employment, economic prosperity, and trade for both the public and private sectors.
- Encourage open communication and cooperation, as well as the spread of information about goods movement.
- Sync the movement of goods with the preservation of cultural heritage, responsible land use, environmental protection, neighborhood preservation, and resource conservation.
- Provide a safe and secure freight transportation system.

5.29 Positioning and growth

When you are the owner of a start-up trucking business, you understand the risks and benefits that come with expanding your company. Startup, growth, maturity, and transition are the four distinct phases that all businesses go through. To ensure low transaction costs and sound financial management, you'll need to put in place solid systems.

5.30 SWOT analysis

A SWOT analysis is a type of assessment that companies can use to identify areas of strength, weakness, opportunities, and threats. Fundamentally, a SWOT analysis allows businesses to get a bird's-eye view of their operations and begin fine-tuning some aspects.

There are some basic factors why you need to undertake your own SWOT.

- You have good knowledge of your company.
- Different SWOT tasks can be assigned to stakeholders with particular business knowledge, like department managers, company leaders, and many others.
- Keeping audits in-house gives you the freedom to complete them as needed.

However, a few more reasons why hiring a professional 3PL to conduct your logistics SWOT analysis is a good idea.

- Allows an independent third-party logistics and supply chain expert to conduct an unbiased analysis.
- Doesn't take up department managers' or other key stakeholders' time, allowing everyone to focus on their jobs.
- The reporting is thorough, comprehensive, and completed quickly. This allows you to identify areas of strength, weakness, opportunity. And threats sooner, and make adjustments to your business with very little delay.

Break down the company strengths

A logistics company's technology, equipment, providing niche services or products, financial resources, and ability to serve customers are all examples of strengths that allow them to accelerate ahead of competitors.

Discover the company weaknesses

Identifying a company's weaknesses is probably the most important task. Many people and businesses find it difficult to look inward to identify areas where they struggle or lack their business. However, in an attempt to optimize, you must first identify the areas in which your company struggles. This is the most crucial part and the most difficult for a logistics company to handle on its own.

Revisit the trucking business opportunities

While strengths and weaknesses serve as a foundation for improvement, the opportunity enables the company to grow and expand in the end. Opportunities for a logistics company can range from improving vendor, supplier, and customer communication platforms to upgrading facilities, equipment, or resources to make them more efficient.

Determine threats

A business threat is anything that gets in the way of your success. It can be financial, structural, competitive, or technological. Due to the numerous threats that exist and fall outside of the expertise of the business stakeholders, this is usually the most difficult area to discover.

Questions to ask yourself

If you're trying to figure out how to finish your SWOT analysis, you must ask a few questions about each segment.

Strengths

- What aspects of your business processes have proven to be fruitful?
- Do you have a variety of assets at your disposal, like networking, education, skills, etc.?

- Which of your physical assets – technology, customers, cash, equipment, or patents – do you own?
- Do you have a distinct advantage over your competitors?

Weaknesses

- What are the areas of your business that need to be improved?
- What resources will you need to improve your competitiveness?
- Are there any openings in your company that need to be filled?
- Is there anything your company needs to stay competitive in?
- What is the overall state of your building? Is it necessary to upgrade or relocate it?

Opportunities

- What areas of your company, if improved, will have the greatest impact and provide the best return on investment?
- Do you have any low-hanging fruit or areas that could be improved?

- Are there any pending regulatory issues that could help your company?
- What is your company's reputation among customers, vendors, suppliers, and other partners, and how can you improve it?

Threats

- Do you have any new or existing competitors in your market?
- Can you gather all of the resources you'll need to keep your supply chain running smoothly?
- Do you have any technological or financial limitations that are preventing you from achieving your goals?
- Is the market poised for expansion, or is it in a state of limbo?

While the questions above will give you a general overview of each segment of the SWOT analysis, it will take a seasoned professional to make an impact on your logistics business and industry truly.

5.31 Pricing Strategy

Prices frequently change in a dynamic pricing strategy. Changes in the product, delivery area or location, increasing or decreasing demand, and changing economic conditions are the most common causes. Several strategy modifications within the realm of dynamic pricing permit freight and logistics businesses to customize pricing to align with profitability goals. The significance of profitable logistics pricing strategies is highlighted by the cumulative impact of intense industry competition and rising transportation costs. Variations of a dynamic pricing structure are among the top choices for developing pricing strategies that can meet the specific customer needs and differing cost-based situations in most businesses. The trucking industry has a wide range of pricing strategies and tactics. While the best strategy for each company differs, revenue management, yield management, penetration, skimming, slip, and geographic pricing are among the most common. This gives businesses the flexibility to select the best options based on their factors or profiles, offer services, marketing objectives, targeted segment, and so on. The most common pricing strategies and tactics can be classified based on the newness of the service provided, such as new services versus existing services. Companies approach pricing for new services with greater caution because they lack experience with the service to base their decisions.

In this regard, it should achieve the following goals:

- The price which is acceptable to prospective customers
- When the competition becomes more intense, price to maintain market share.
- The set price must allow for a profit.

The following are the most common trucking business pricing strategies based on these goals:

Penetration strategy

Typically, when a new service is introduced to the market using a price penetration strategy, it is supported by intense promotion services such as advertising, discounts, etc. It entails charging a low price for a new service to ensure rapid consumer acceptance. When there is intense market competition, many similar services, and opportunities for distinctiveness are limited, this strategy is recommended.

Skimming strategy

When there is little or no market competition, or when there is a market segment of consumers willing to pay a high price for high-quality services, and research and development costs or input market costs are significant, this strategy is used. It entails charging a high price for a new service to get a quick return on investment for the development and launch of the product and make a profit.

This strategy allows you to reduce the price at any time to increase sales volume and profit.

Slip strategy

It's a variation of the skimming strategy, which entails determining the "slip" demand curve by launching a new service at a high price and then lowering the price before the competition because of technological advances. The company can achieve the highest sales volume while discouraging competitors by lowering prices faster than the competition.

This strategy involves the emergence and intensification of competition in the market following the introduction of the service, but it can also be used to attract a broader segment of consumers even if there is no competition.

Revenue and Yield Management

Less-than-full truckload haulers frequently use revenue management pricing. In addition to basing prices on the destination point, revenue management works to maximize profits by setting the price based on the percentage of a full truckload the merchandise occupies or charging the full truckload rate regardless of the space merchandise occupies if the customer prefers.

Perishable goods transporters frequently use a yield management pricing strategy to set prices depending on the need for quick, timely delivery.

Variables such as changing established routes and drivers to get a load delivered in a reasonable amount of time are reflected in prices.

5.32 Geographical Pricing

Long-haul companies frequently use geographical pricing. Within the prices customers pay, a geographical pricing strategy enables freight and logistics businesses to account for changes in fuel costs, vehicle wear and tear, driver wages, and, in some cases, liability.

A common example is zone pricing, which sets different prices for different geographic locations depending on the location from a warehouse or other shipping site.

Short-haul or local freight businesses can use a uniform delivery pricing variation, which charges the same price to every customer, though it is less common.

Pricing and its significance

The pricing strategies of successful trucking companies are similar. Above all, successful businesses set prices that reflect the value of their goods and services.

Logistics companies that use reflective pricing strategies typically have profit margins 17 percent higher than their competitors.

Furthermore, successful logistics companies commit to developing effective pricing strategies and enforcing strict guidelines that prevent salespeople from adjusting prices to meet sales quotas.

5.33 Top and effective ways to market your trucking business

New customers are essential for running a successful trucking business and thriving in the trucking industry. The growth of your trucking business necessitates the employment of tailor-made marketing strategies for the trucking industry. It would help if you reached out to your target audience. This could be conceived as a time-consuming job, but you will not succeed if you rely only on basic marketing strategies and won't broaden your customer base. The marketing strategies mentioned below are just a few of the many you can employ to promote your trucking business. Many businesses require trucking services. Your core task is to identify and target your customers using ingenious marketing tactics. Using traditional marketing techniques to grow a trucking company, such as load boards, will make it extremely difficult for you to promote and project your trucking company. As a trucker, the best way to make money is to go out and find your customers and shippers to work with on a long-term basis. Practical marketing tips for truckers are listed below to help them lure in customers and expand their business.

Trucking Load Boards

You must identify and approach your customers when you are working on marketing your trucking company. Trucking load boards are made for both trucking companies and consumers who need transportation. The websites listed below make it simple to promote your company. These also assist you in connecting with consumers who are looking for your services. Users will be able to search in two ways on the following websites. To begin, as a transportation company owner, you can look for loads which need to be moved. Customers can also go to the website and look for trucks in their area to pick up a load. This service is available at the following websites:

- Direct Freight Services
- Truls
- Freight Finder
- Landstar Carriers
- Trucker Path
- 123 Load Board
- Truckers Edge

5.34 Partner with Trade Publications

Numerous businesses advertise in trade publications because of their highly targeted audiences. For example, Truck Parts and Service, CCJ, Overdrive, and Successful Dealer are some trade publications working in the trucking industry and offering well-defined, segmented audiences. Many trade publications (including the ones mentioned above) have digital components. This helps these trade publications in providing you with digital advertising that is displayed to these audiences online. Whereas these publications are recognized for their print editions, their digital editions can greatly add to the trucking company's marketing campaign. You can geo-target your banner and newsletter ads, just like the rest of your digital advertising. This will help you astutely target the market segment most likely to gain from your products and services. You can create comprehensive online advertising campaigns by collaborating with multi-channel brands that offer highly targeted audiences. The display network provides you with a fantastic opportunity to target the audience and switch them through creative advertising. Print ads provide an excellent opportunity for targeting your customers, just like online marketing tools in the trucking industry. Industry-specific trade publications are intended to inform readers about current trucking trends. The advantage of placing ads in these publications is that you'll be sure to reach an interested audience looking for trucking information. It would help if you considered the efficacy of trade publications in your decision-making about the placement of your ads. If you're looking for new drivers, for example, you could advertise in trucking industry publications. If you're selling services, consider placing ads in publications that cater to the industries you serve. Find trade publications with the audience you're looking for using this database of trade publications organized by industry. Several trade publications have an online component. This should help you in devising your marketing strategy. While many subscribers prefer industry magazines in print, many others will read the publication online. Investment in digital advertising helps you to target your business market effectively.

Join trade associations and attend their events

Trade associations are dedicated and well-organized in the provision of education and networking opportunities to their members. The trade associations' prime objective is to help them grow their businesses. You must reach out to trade publications for advice and implementation of your marketing strategy. By visiting these trade publications, you will get an opportunity to gain more insight into the trucking industry. You will also get an opportunity to share some of your marketing materials. Make a set of business cards, magnets, or flyers for distribution. You would be able to get in touch with a unique technique to incorporate into your marketing strategy. It would help if you tried to make connections with relevant people. Trade associations, like trade publications, provide an opportunity to connect with a receptive audience. You could, for example, establish a booth at a trucking industry trade expo for recruiting new drivers. If you're trying to sell your services to other businesses, you should go to B2B events. To attract customers, create a visually appealing and informative display. You should carry this material to a trade expo for distributing these marketing materials to the participants. You need to be aware that exhibiting at a trade show is costly and time-consuming. Consider becoming a sponsor if you don't have the expertise and time to create an eye-catching display. You can put your advertisements on promotional materials, on-site advertising, and put your marketing materials in swag bags. Attendees will remember your business if they need transportation services in the future because of your advertisements. You should also look into the online component of such events. You have to find out about the organization's facility for advertisements on the registration site. When you place advertisements on such sites, your company will be automatically introduced to each vendor to who they sign up.

Take advantage of social media by using sponsored social media posts

The trade publications, industry boards, and events make it easy to find customers on the lookout for transportation services. However, social media gives you an excellent opportunity to reach out to potential trucking customers. Remember that you will have to use social media for the best results for marketing your trucking business. Create and use profiles, particularly on LinkedIn and Facebook. Customers will trust you more if you have accounts. It also provides them with another way to contact you. You can use social media sites like Facebook, Twitter, Instagram, and LinkedIn to promote your business, share your shipping rates, and provide a link to your company's website to interested buyers for future business. Consider running paid ads on social media to get the most out of your trucking company. You can reach out to the audience based on their geographic location, profession, and interest in the trucking industry whenever you create a sponsored post. You have to ensure the provision of correct information when creating your profile or profiles. Customers will need information regarding your address, website address (if applicable), and phone number. Ensure that the furnished information is consistent across all your social media profiles if you have more than one. Share photos, updates, and special offers with those who follow your company on social media. It encourages more people to participate. Plus, if you provide excellent service, your customers can rate you on social media and strongly recommend you to others.

5.35 How to establish a business niche and brand image?

Starting a profitable business or, to put it another way, becoming your boss does not necessitate obtaining all of the necessary certifications or college degrees; it all boils down to your resilience and commitment to achieving your goals. This can be accomplished by collecting valuable information and knowledge about the trucking industry. Although some businesses require certifications, licenses, and college degrees to start, the truth is that there are plenty of businesses that you can start with just what you have, and one of these businesses is an owner-operator trucking business. If you have your truck, this business is ideal for you. All you have to do now is ensure that you have the necessary commercial driver's license (CDL), business network, and attitude. One of the advantages of the industry is that it is open to willing entrepreneurs. An owner-operator trucking company requires a modest amount of startup capital, and the amount of money you can make depends on how hard you can work because clients will always need your services. Most owner-operators work 24 hours a day, seven days a week, and rarely take a break. You have to market your business, execute your job and keep your customers satisfied. You are the owner, and you have to take responsibility for all work. One of the advantages of owning a trucking company would be that the owner trucking operator has the option of working as a freelancer without having to sign a retainer agreement with a company, or they can sign a lease agreement with a firm of their choice and commit to the organization for a set period.

Furthermore, the above-mentioned agreements may be renewed. You want to establish an owner-operator trucking firm and develop a business specialty, build brand recognition, and target the appropriate market. In such a situation, you should keep the following suggestions in mind.

Understand the industry

The trucking industry has become an essential and integral part of the world economy. Moreover, and owner-trucking business also works in the same vital trucking industry. They transport large quantities of dirt, raw materials, rocks, machines, equipment, building materials, and finished goods over land. These things are transported from production facilities to retail distribution centers. They also transport materials from warehouses to construction sites. Thus the trucking industry offers essential services to the US economy. Heavy-duty trucks are, in fact, essential in the construction industry. The trucking industry is a major stakeholder in the manufacturing, transportation, and warehousing industries in the United States of America and other parts of the world. According to statistics, food and food products, lumber or wood products, petroleum, or coal account for 34.8 % of truck traffic in the US. Additionally, clay, glass, concrete and stone, farm products, and petroleum, and coal account for 35.6 % of truck traffic by volume. The development of technology in areas such as computers, satellite communication, and the internet has greatly aided the industry's growth. Technology has increased the productivity of trucking companies' operations by allowing them to monitor their trucks and drivers better and allow drivers to save time and effort. Moreover, the trucking industry is also responsible for the majority of freight movement over land. Smaller trucks help transport smaller quantities of goods from one location within a city to another location within the same city. The trucking industry is not limited to trailers or large trucks transporting goods from destination to destination via interstate highways. The trucking industry is about more than just transporting goods over long distances. In fact, in the United States, about 66 percent of truck tonnage travels less than 100 miles; local and regional hauls account for nearly half of all truck revenues, and they are the preferred mode of transport for private carriers. Without a doubt, establishing and running an owner-operator trucking company can be difficult, but the truth is that it can also be rewarding. One of the advantages of the industry is that it is open to both big-time investors with the financial means to launch a fleet of trucks and aspiring entrepreneurs with just one truck. Even though the trucking industry includes both small operators with a single truck and large operators with fleets of trucks spread across the United States, the industry is not fully saturated in any way. The need to transport materials from one destination to another will increase so the owner-operator trucking businesses will always have a ready market.

Conduct market research and feasibility studies for understanding demographics and psychographics

Construction companies and building material sales companies do not constitute the demographic and psychographic composition of those hiring owner-operator trucking companies. A wide range of corporate and individual clients cannot move their goods, machines, equipment, or dirt without the assistance of a standard and licensed owner-operator truck company. Merchants and warehouse operators, retailers who would like to move the goods from one location to another, manufacturers (chemical manufacturers, textile manufacturers, and so on), households who want to move from one apartment to another, and corporate organizations who want to move from one office to another should all be included in the target market of owner operator trucking companies.

Employ niche marketing strategy

Establishing a solid reputation as a dependable service provider is one of the challenges for new owner-operators. Shippers want assurance that their loads will arrive safely. Small and new brokerage firms have quite a way of addressing these concerns while also boosting their earning potential in the first year. They identify a market segment that larger companies have overlooked or ignored, specializing in serving that group. It's known as niche marketing, and it's the simplest way to start a brokerage business.

Advantages of marketing to a narrower niche

Targeting a specific market segment allows you to develop a unique customer profile, allowing you to craft messages that hit their emotional hot buttons each time you communicate with them. You get more positive responses and business as your messaging aligns with their pain and pleasure centers.

How to choose a market niche?

Before obtaining the proper knowledge of the trucking business, some people already know which markets to target. Others are less fortunate and must begin from the ground up. If you fall into the latter category, you have two options for selecting a market niche:

- Evaluate your skills, talents, interests, and personality to see how they will play a role in your freight broker business; or
- Research the industry's segmentations, pick a specialty, and learn everything you can about serving that sector.

Find a niche that you enjoy while also having sufficient potential for growth to sustain the business over time. For example, some owner-operators specialize in market niches and segments linked to their passions and interests, such as antiques, microchips, or automobiles. You can set yourself apart from the competition by focusing on a niche that you're passionate about and providing can-do, bend-over-backward service. And you know what they say: a satisfied customer is a happy customer, and a repeat customer is a happy customer.

Owner-operator niches

There are many ways to locate the market niche and find customers. Given below are some techniques that you can use in finding the captive market and growing your business:

- Concentrating on regional niches. Customers can be found in your immediate area, whether it's in your city or state. Your location could be a beehive of manufacturing for automobiles, microchips, semiconductors, and other goods.
- If you're passionate about automobiles, you're likely to know a lot about their manufacturers and have easy access to a primary contact who can put you in touch with the decision-makers. Ensure you can expand with these customers rather than spreading yourself too thin—your enthusiasm should align your capability, so you don't ruin your reputation by not handling the loads.
- Providing niche services based on the type of trucks used. Everything from dry vans to flatbeds to tankers to dump trailers and everything in between. You can choose to concentrate your efforts on one or multiple kinds of trucks to find shippers more quickly.

- Brokering cargo that requires special attention. When you concentrate on a single type of load, such as dairy, you can quickly address issues such as truck type, climate specifications, shipper preferences, and so on.
- When you serve a specific niche for a long time, you become an expert in that niche. Before you know it, you've established yourself as the go-to guy for only certain types of cargo in your space. You can bet that once you've developed a reputation for solid dependability, expanding your market or your reach will be much easier.

Niche Marketing Tips

Before you can implement a successful niche marketing strategy, you must first identify your niche. Consider your service area. Which industries are underserved? Distribute questionnaires to the professional network or group. Speak with local businesses about the carrier service and consider how you might compete for their business. Before you go too far with your business, start small. To begin developing your strategy, conduct a comparative assessment of your regional competitors and employ the following techniques:

- Use Your Experience as a Niche
- Build a Healthy Portfolio
- Attract more Clients

- Attract different Clients
- Expand your business
- Link Up with Other Professionals
- Utilize Advanced Technology
- Promote Your Specialty

Challenges in niche marketing

However, there is a risk in niche marketing: you may become so centered that your net income comes from only a few sources. Learn from the trucking industry's specialty haulers. They don't get more than 25% -30% of their revenue from a single source, and they keep it diversified within the niche. With the economy's ups and downs, putting all your eggs in one basket can spell disaster if something goes wrong... Even large freight brokerage firms are not immune to this reality. The trucking industry is one of many heavily regulated by the federal government and issues licenses. Most owner-operated trucking companies provide general services that a typical owner-operated trucking company would provide, and owner-operated trucking is a niche market in the trucking industry. However, some owner operator trucking companies may choose to specialize in certain areas, such as local and long-distance transportation of construction materials, machines, equipment, dirt, rocks, and building materials, transportation of construction and agricultural equipment, and transportation of oil and gas waste products

Conduct economic analysis

If your objective is to earn money, accomplish business growth, pursue expansion, and make a national name, you, as an owner-operator trucking business, must conduct proper economic research and analysis and consider all factors that constitute the cost side of your business. When it comes to cost and economic analysis for your owner-operator trucking business, three key factors must be considered: location, pricing, and promotion. While managing your owner-operator trucking business, you'll need to keep reviewing these key factors regularly. Suppose you want to maximize profits and be at the forefront of the industry as an operator trucking business owner. In that case, you must have a thorough understanding of your competitive landscape. It's worth noting that truck fueling, servicing, and maintenance costs are some of the most significant contributors to the cumulative cost of an owner-operator trucking business, and they should be factored into your costing and economic analysis.

The level of competition in the industry

Whatever line of business you choose, you will face competition from others, including the government, who are in the same industry as you. Thus there are no exceptions for an owner-operator trucking business. The competitive rivalry in the owner-operator trucking industry is influenced by the location of the business, the niche area of operation, and, of course, the truck's capacity. You will likely face little or no competition if you somehow skillfully develop a distinctive niche for the owner-operator trucking business. For example, suppose you have a monopoly in your area in that you collect radioactive waste and haul it locally. In that case, you can dominate the market for a long time before the emergence of any competition. It's also worth noting that the truck's capacity determines competition in the owner-operator trucking line of business and the trucking industry.

Know your major competitors in the Industry

It is a fact that certain brands perform better or are conceived better by customers and the general public as compared to other brands in every industry. Some of these companies have a long history in the industry, while others are best known for conducting business. Moreover, their results and achievements stand out in the industry. Listed below are some of the most well-known owner-operators and trucking companies in the United States and worldwide.

- Sierra West Express
- Sinclair Trucking Company

- Southeastern Freight Lines
- Swift Transportation
- Consolidated Freightways
- PRO Transport, Inc.
- Con-way Truckload
- Schneider National
- Covenant Transport
- Daseke Inc.
- USF Glen Moore
- Knight Transportation
- YRC Worldwide
- US Express
- Amodio Van and Storage
- Shaffer Trucking
- Werner Enterprises

Know the possible threats and challenges you will face

One of the major challenges you will most likely face if you plan to start your own owner-operator trucking business today is the presence of well-established owner-operator trucking businesses in your chosen target market. This problem can be avoided if you develop your market, focus on households, individuals, and small construction businesses that require trucking services. Mature markets, economic recession and downturn, fierce competition, highly unstable costs, and rising fuel prices are some of the other threats and challenges you'll likely face when starting your owner-operator trucking business. Adverse government policies, demographic and social factors, seasonal fluctuations, an economic downturn that will likely affect consumer spending, and, of course, the emergence of new competitors in your target market's location are all factors that need to be considered. It isn't much you can do about these threats and challenges except remain hopeful that things will remain favorable for your business.

Choose a catchy business name

When you decide to give a name to your trucking company, you should usually be creative because the name you choose will go a long way toward establishing a perception of what the company represents. When it comes to naming a business, it is common for people to follow the industry's trend in which they intend to operate. Here are some catchy names to consider if you're thinking about beginning your own owner operator trucking company:

- Walcott Ron Owner Trucking Company
- Rodney James Owner Trucking Company
- Silva Pearson Owner Trucking Company
- Glaziers Brothers Trucking Company
- Ferguson Tony & Sons Owner Trucking Services

- Johnson Pedro Owner Trucking Company
- Alexis Gunter® Owner Trucking Company
- Leo Marvin & Sons Owner Trucking Company
- Mike Lawrence Owner Trucking Company
- Charles Lance Owner Trucking Company

Protect your intellectual property with trademarks, copyrights, patents

You might not be compelled to file for intellectual property or trademark rights if you contemplate starting your own operator trucking business. This is because the business nature allows you to run it successfully without ever having to go to court to sue someone for using your company's intellectual property rights without permission.

Develop strategies to boost brand awareness and create a corporate identity

Suppose your goal for starting an owner-operator trucking business is to grow it from a one-man operation to a full-fledged trucking company that is composed of fleets of trucks moving goods across the United States. In that case, you'll need to be willing to spend money on brand promotion and advertising. Whatever industry you're in, the truth is that the market is constantly changing, and you'll need to ensure constant brand awareness and use effective marketing strategies to keep your name in front of your target market and keep them engaged. Here are some of the platforms you can use to increase brand awareness and establish a corporate identity for the owner-operator trucking company:

- Make effective use of print and electronic media platforms like magazines, newspapers, etc.
- Through selective sponsoring of community-based events
- Make effective use of the internet and social media platforms like; Instagram, Facebook, Twitter, YouTube, Google + et al. for promotion of your trucking company business
- By installing billboards on strategic locations with a maximum traffic count
- By distributing fliers and handbills in target areas
- Reach out to construction sites, farmers, corporate organizations, manufacturers and retailers of machines and equipment, and demolition and wreckage companies in your target areas. You can achieve this by making use of mobile phone service. You can brief them about your business and the associated services
- By listing your owner-operator trucking business in local directories
- By advertising the owner-operator trucking business on your official website

- By employing strategies that could help you in pulling traffic to the site
- By making your staff wear branded shirts
- By proper branding of your truck with excellent placement of your trucking company's logo

CHAPTER 6:

Managing Human Resource and Building Fleet for Trucking Business

This chapter will discuss the various details ancillary to running a trucking business like hiring drivers and workforce, building a fleet, reaching out to customers, and managing finances through effective expense management techniques.

6.1 Managing your business finances and raising the desired start-up capital

If you already own a haulage truck, then planning on a new owner-operator trucking company will have minimal cost implications for you.

A large portion of your startup capital is usually spent on securing a haulage truck. As a result, if you decide to start up a business without having a haulage truck, you may not need to raise funds to finance it. One of the first things you should think about business financing is writing a good business plan.

You may not have to work as hard to persuade your bank, investors, or friends to invest in your business if you develop a logical and detailed financial proposal for the said purpose.

When looking for initial capital for the owner-operator trucking business, consider the following options:

- Raising funds from personal savings and the sale of personal stocks and properties
- Raising funds from investors and business partners
- Selling shares to interested investors
- Obtaining a bank loan

- Pitching the business idea as well as applying for business grants from the government, donor organizations, and angel investors
- Securing soft loans from friends and family members

Besides, you also need to take into consideration the following:

Ensure your customers are paying you for the loads you haul

You can't handle your cash flow if you don't have a predictable source of income. Two factors must be considered here: whether or not your clients will pay and when. You have no way of knowing your potential clients and brokers' payment history or if they pay their bills on time unless you run credit checks on them. Conducting credit checks is the simplest way for determining if the goods being hauled by you are for the clients who have a good credit and payment history. The good news for owner-operators is that financial partners are available, like certain freight bill factoring companies that provide free credit checks to their factoring clients, allowing them to save money while ensuring they are paid. However, keep in mind that the timing of your clients' payments has an impact on your cash flow. It is not uncommon for freight bills to take 30, 60, or even 90 days to be paid. However, during the said time, your bills continue to accumulate.

Partnering with a freight bill factoring company is one way to eliminate payment terms uncertainty. Freight bill factoring provides you with immediate access to freight bills, allowing you to pay your bills when you need to.

Accurately track expenses and get the help you need when you need it

The only way to truly understand your cash flow situation is to track your income and expenses accurately. This could very well become difficult when you spend a lot of time on the road. There are a few options available to you, based on your comfort level and the amount of time you could afford to devote to financial matters.

- Some fuel management programs could indeed track fuel spending. These also include fuel management tools and purchase controls that help you monitor and track your fuel and other expenses.
- Some freight bill factoring companies provide free back-office services like invoicing, processing, postage, etc.
- Professional accounting and bookkeeping services are available for owner-operators who require professional services for handling their accounts.

Look for ways to save money

You will not be worried about your cash flow if you have the habit of retaining money and, at the same time, do not spend it on non-productive matters. Owner-operators can save money in a variety of ways. In addition to providing the financial tools mentioned above, fuel programs are also a great way to save money. You can save up to ten cents per gallon with fuel cards, and there are no minimum fueling requirements. You also get the cash price if you use the facility of paying with a card. You can also load your funds directly onto your fuel card if you work with a freight bill factoring company. You can save time and, at the same time, ensure that you have sufficient funds to cover your fuel costs. Many owner-operators are looking for ways to save money and increase cash flow overlook equipment leasing. A seasoned leasing company can provide a variety of options to tailor a solution to your specific needs. Leasing options could include ways to reduce your payments, assist you in getting upgraded equipment that saves you money on maintenance and fuel, and repayment plans that account for seasonality changes in the business. There can be no single solution that could be applied to manage your cash flow problems. You will have a smoother financial ride if you can stay ahead of any potential problems.

6.2 Choose a suitable location for your business

Starting a trucking business as an owner-operator is simple and easy; it is a business that can be started in any location. Several owner-operator trucking businesses operate from the comfort of their homes, particularly if they have ample parking in their compound. It cannot be overemphasized that the location you choose to start your owner-operator trucking business is critical to its success. As a result, entrepreneurs prefer to rent or lease a facility in a visible location. They prefer locations occupied by many individuals and businesses with the required purchasing power; and a location with minimal obstacles to overcome about securing permits and licenses. Suppose you rent or lease a facility for your owner-operator trucking business in a difficult-to-reach location with difficult terrain. In that case, you should expect to pay more for fuel and maintenance of your haulage truck. It is important to remember that the price of a business facility in a good location will have a significant impact on your overall costs, so you should be able to set aside enough money in your budget to lease or rent packing space.

6.3 Expense Management

A few of the responsibilities you'll have to deal with include overseeing the loading and unloading process, planning the routes that are safe for you and your drivers, and communicating with dispatch. Moreover, you will also have to effectively monitor and accurately document all activities associated with your company. Understanding the business and effectively managing the associated expenses is one of the most important factors in running an owner-operator trucking company business. You must know how to prioritize your finances. This is especially true if you work for yourself. Your company could face a financial crisis if it is not properly managed, which could affect your job security and that of your employees. The magnitude of your trucking business's expenses will vary depending on your company's unique services, but the actual costs you'll want to keep track of are:

- the cost of the trucks themselves
- the fuel you use to power them
- the general market and weather considerations
- roadblocks

Here are some tips and guidelines to help you save money and get useful management tools when you need them.

Inspection and maintenance

It is worth mentioning that effective and timely truck maintenance can help you save money on unnecessary maintenance and repairs. If your trucks are used frequently and are expected to last for a long time, you must watch any minor issues that could turn into a major headache. The following factors should be closely monitored and optimized regularly:

Tires

If your tires aren't properly inflated, it will directly impact your vehicle's fuel efficiency.

Oil levels

If your truck is not lubricated appropriately and on time, then the engine could overheat. This could then result in costly replacement or repair.

Exterior Features

You may be forced to spend a significant amount of money on replacing a large external piece of the truck's body if you fail to acknowledge even the smallest dents and scratches. The lights, brakes, and wiring must be checked regularly. You should also check radiator fluid levels regularly.

Fuel-saving methods

Fuel is the most expensive part of your overall cost. This is very unfortunate; given that it is such an important part of your business. As a result, you may want to look for ways to cut your fuel costs as much as possible.

Some of the tips given below can help you reduce this expensive cost item in your trucking business:

- You must get a fuel card with a discount. These cards can help trucking companies save fuel by paying the reduced price at the pump and providing other useful features and capabilities for owner-operators.
- You and your driver need to drive at a speed compatible with safety. This is because driving at high speed can result in increased fuel consumption.
- You must keep track of your truck's idle time and keep it to a minimum. When you're waiting for the drive-thru takeaway food, it might be cold without the heater on, but this can eat up your gas.
- Always use the appropriate fuel for the truck.
- Having invested in roof fairing is also a good idea.
- Improve your truck's aerodynamics: When your truck is facing air resistance, much fuel is wasted.
- You should use the air conditioner when necessary.

Invest in a Transport Management System (TMS)

The logistics of a company's operations can be perplexing as well as overwhelming at times. As a result, it might be a good idea to invest in a TMS. Simply put, the analytical data provided by the said platform allows you to track and monitor all logistical elements of the business. This service assists you in properly organizing functions like drop-off times and cost-effective, safe, and timely travel. Other features and benefits include:

- Supply costs
- Freight costs
- Real-time tracking of cargo location
- Route-schedule facility
- Invoice production
- Optimal use of supply chain network (travel time estimations, status updates)
- Business statistics
- Timely reporting.

Ensure you understand your expenses

If you understand your truck's operating costs, you will be able to figure out the cost-cutting options and situations. There are some fixed costs like permits, licenses, labor costs, and insurance. On the contrary, some variable costs depend largely on your usage. The variable costs include fuel, tolls, and maintenance requirements. You should also take into consideration coffee and food breaks and expenses.

Budgeting

After you have developed a better understanding of your operating expenditures, you will be available with the right information required for the effective budgeting of your business. Monthly budgeting would allow you to allocate money to every relevant business area properly. Failing to budget appropriately will end up in you losing money on your trucking company business. Consequently, you will fail to finance the direly needed aspects of your management features.

Route planning

If you map out the best route for your drivers, you will overcome unnecessary spending. If you have the skills and expertise by which you can make use of the right apps and internet searches, you should be facilitated in finding and avoiding the following elements:

- Stations that have higher fuel prices
- Expected detours
- Unanticipated accidents
- Traffic clogging
- Alternate routes
- Inclement weather conditions
- Road construction work delays.

Protect your cargo from theft

An alarming concern for an owner-operator trucking company is the goods that are stolen from the cargo. Thieves are creative and can steal from your freight cargo. This can cost them massively. The drivers, as well as the owner-operators, should be aware of this problem. They should also develop systems whereby they can introduce preventive mechanisms for avoiding such thefts. Listed below are some of the prevention methods that may benefit an owner-operator:

- Figure out the type of goods that are frequently stolen.
- Determine the locations where thefts are likely to occur along with the timings of theft.
- You should park your truck at a safe location. It is suggested to park in areas where you can check and restrict any unwanted entries. You should avoid parking in unsafe areas. Try to park your vehicle near security cameras.
- You should be active enough to notice any suspicious driving activity. If you believe that you will be followed, you must reach out to your manager for help. You should try your left best to lose the suspicious followers safely while driving.

- You should wise use your efficient safety gear: This could include padlocks, alarms, and other security programs.
- You have to make sure that you are working with trustworthy people.
- You should be very careful in the selection of your transportation partners.
- Security training for employees is strongly recommended.
- Security guards need to be hired at base locations.

6.4 Choose your market niche wisely

Based on the industry in which your trucking company operates, you'll need to invest in specific equipment and set the overall rates accordingly. You should wisely choose and work in a niche that, theoretically, pays better than others. For example, dry van transportation isn't considered a lucrative trucking niche. Fresh produce and meat transportation, on the other hand, is kind of invulnerable to recessions and is thought to be less competitive because it is relevant all year. Other lucrative markets to consider are:

- Hazmat (hazardous materials)
- Tankers
- Luxury cars
- Over-sized loads
- Mining industry.

6.5 Know when to outsource and insource business functions

Trying to manage every aspect of your business on your own or with your internal team can be exhausting. This technique is also not very cost-efficient. For many owner-operators, time and money are two major concerns. Suppose you could somehow outsource specific functions to other companies, like a Professional Employer Organization (PEO). In that case, you might be better off in the long run and have more time to focus on the most important aspects of your company. These businesses can handle the following:

- Safety and health management
- Training
- Development programs
- Employee benefits
- Payroll
- Worker's compensation

However, if you decide to outsource several business operations that you can better manage yourself, you may be wasting money. You should have trust and belief in your human resource abilities and skills in managing your business successfully.

6.6 Final thoughts

It's difficult enough to run your own trucking company without the added stress of financial control and safety. You might believe that filling up your trucks with low-cost fuel or outsourcing all of the business functions will fix all of your cost issues. However, there are several other cost-cutting options that you may want to consider to keep the expenses as low as possible. It's a good idea to make sure you know where you're spending your money, whether it's on maintenance or something else, and to be aware of even the smallest actions you and the team could take to cut down on unnecessary spending.

Building your fleet

Have you ever stopped on the side of the road thinking about how you could take more control of your career by becoming your boss and running your own trucking company? Many have, but most of them do not realize their dreams because they rush into them without planning. You can't expect to become a business owner in a short period and expect to have a 100-truck fleet by Friday. Commitment, perseverance, planning, and hard work are the personality features required to fulfill your dreams. Starting and running your own business isn't easy, particularly in an industry like trucking, where many new small fleet owners don't make it past the second year. However, the good news is that trucking businesses could still be considered a thriving industry because the shipping industry is constantly expanding as more and more products are moved around the world. It's contingent upon how you run your business and what steps you take to transform it into a successful and lucrative business. Given below are some tips to help you get started on the road to realizing your trucking dreams.

6.7 Plan ahead

It's in human nature to act or do things without thinking about them. Anyone can decide to join the ranks of the small fleet owners and begin operating a trucking company on a given day. What would you do if you were in that situation? Do you have any idea where you need to go? Have you worked out the investment capital that would be needed to start the business? Do you have any idea how much money you'll make? What type of trucking insurance is best for you? Are you going to lease or operate your trucks and find loads from load boards? If you're going to lease, which company will you choose to lease the trucking fleet from, and how much will you pay? There are too many aspects that you must consider and think about before making any decision. So, if you're planning on starting your own trucking company, then you must avoid unwise and hasty decisions. If you want to establish a small trucking company, you'll need a road map. Yes, we understand that sitting down to write a good business plan and a cash flow plan is tedious and theoretical. However, doing so is critical for the business and credit score, and your well-being. Planning and writing down what you need to do gives you a better understanding of the various aspects of starting and running a business. It's similar to a map that directs you to your destination. It also gives you a hint about whether you'll have a consistent cash flow to support your family.

Slow and steady wins the race

Many truckers start small and want to expand far too quickly. So they go out and purchase a truckload of trucks, only to become overwhelmed and collapse in a short time. They could ward off such a situation only by timely planning and patience. Before expanding your fleet, consider whether it is imperative and whether your finances allow it. After careful consideration and calculation, if you determine that it is time to expand your trucking company, then start small with one truck. This way, your adjustments won't be as significant, and you'll be able to keep up with the pace. There's also the consideration that you want to ensure that the drivers are qualified and will protect your assets. This, however, will take time. Some people recommend taking a test drive with the drivers before hiring them so you can see how they operate. This also allows you to rectify their mistakes. People also propose to hire the driver in the first phase and then get a truck for them. We recommend that you start by looking within your existing network to see if you can find an experienced driver. This gives you a sense of security because you know the person, but you must still be cautious and take the same precautions as your other drivers. Take your time. The most critical decision in starting a trucking company is about the hiring of a truck driver. You need to do your research and make sure the person you're hiring is the right person for your company.

No deal is better than a bad deal

The American Trucking Association (ATA) predicted a 4.2 percent increase in transportation volume in 2018 and a 2.3 percent annual growth rate from 2019 to 2024 in August 2018. This indicates that the trucking industry is thriving and has good prospects.

However, this could also indicate that an increasing number of people want to start their own trucking company. This would translate into intense competition in the industry. As a result of the fierce competition, some owner-operators are lowering their rates. This, however, should not be the way forward in a competitive business. As a business owner, you are well aware of the value of the service you provide. If you're confident in your ability to provide excellent service, reducing your rates shouldn't be one of your top priorities.

will gladly pay you at your rate if your company is known for providing high-quality service. But you must continue to operate efficiently if you charge a premium price. Although price competition cannot be avoided, many customers would rather pay more for better service than suffer the consequences of poor service. So, if you believe a job offer isn't going to be profitable for you, it's okay to say no and decline it.

When it comes to profitability, make sure you don't just look at the amount of money you make. One offer may appear to be more valuable than the other at first glance, but when you do the simple arithmetic, you'll find that it isn't. For example, Deal B offers $600 for a one-day job, while Deal C offers $900 for a shipment that will require a layover. Moreover, you will be required to travel different distances for the latter deal. Deal B may be more appealing based on the demand you have. Don't just look at the dollar amount; look at what's behind it as well. Use other metrics to ensure you're getting the best deal, such as revenue/mile/per hour.

6.8 Develop a loyal customer base

You must be aware of the distinctive features of your business and service as an owner-operator. It's because knowing what sets you apart from your competitors can help you figure out what your customers value. And because you know what makes you stand out, you'll keep doing it – or you'll be inspired to offer more, which will result in repeat customers. You will begin to build a solid customer base by providing a service that your customers will appreciate. And, as with any business, having a strong and loyal customer base would then help you maintain consistent revenue during difficult economic times. These happy and loyal customers will spread the word about your business. This will result in the influx of new customers and help you to grow. However, make sure you don't accept any customer solely to expand as quickly as possible, as this could be potentially lethal. "The ultimate objective is to get freight directly from a shipper. It will pay more and be more consistent.

6.9 Remember it is a business

You are the sole proprietor of your trucking company, which means you are in charge of everything. So, to run a successful trucking business, you must start learning about the industry and join any class that could help you gain insight into the trucking business. After all, you're running a business, which is very different from driving, so learning new skills could be extremely beneficial. You should have experienced human resources to help you conduct your business successfully.

6.10 Hiring drivers and other employees

As a business owner, you can make major investment decisions. At the same time, you can also hire a general manager and task him to operate the company and advise you on critical decisions. You have the prerogative and discretion to induct human resources who are more qualified and sharp than you. You should have the skill and expertise to hire the right people for the right job. This gives you an e opportunity to learn from them and gives you the time to allow smart people to run your business for you and make important decisions. You can then utilize your skills and apply them appropriately in making a score of decisions.

Regarding the number of employees, you'll need to start the business. You don't need to hire anyone; it's a business that the owner can run entirely. The proprietor can work as a driver, marketer, accountant, and logistics manager. However, there will be times when you will be compelled to hire laborers to assist you in loading and unloading your trucks and experts to assist you with some job functions such as truck servicing, repair, and maintenance. If you're just starting, you might not have the financial resources or the necessary business structure to hire all of the professionals you'll need, especially a maintenance team, which is why you should consider entering into a partnership with industry experts.

6.11 How to find your customers?

You must identify high-ticket trucking clients who ship regularly. Look for reputable shippers who require regular deliveries, pay promptly, and have freight lanes that correspond to your ideal routes. It's also a good idea to look for shippers who have quick-paying offers. Pharmaceuticals, food retail stores, auto dealerships, the US Government (one of the country's largest shippers), and many others could be your prospective customers. Take some time to research these local businesses. Focus your energy on unserved businesses and see what you can do to meet their cargo transportation requirements. The membership lists with contact information for most of these organizations are also available publicly, so use them to compile a list of prospects. Once you have them, contact their fleet managers by phone or email to arrange a meeting, preferably in person. Next, learn how they select their carriers and drivers and how you can become one of their best-preferred partners.

6.12 How to sell your service?

Finding new customers is a difficult part of the trucking business for most truckers. Shippers are hesitant to reach a new trucking company. Similarly, they usually do not get a lucrative long-term contract for a good lane from a single call. It will take a consistent effort on your part. Moreover, you will have to focus on your contacts at least once a week. A good customer relations management (CRM) program is essential. Insightly is a tool that you can use. Insightly is a fantastic CRM program for keeping track of your customer relationships. It could be accessed from any location, including your home, office. Even when you are on the road, you can utilize CRM. It is an excellent tool for keeping track of all of your contacts and customers.

6.13 Create a customer lead list

There are numerous methods for compiling a list of prospective customers. If you're running a small business, don't go looking for the area's largest manufacturer. They don't want a small contractor; they want a large corporation to work on a large scale. Even if you succeed in getting an abnormal load from them now and then, chances are you'll be overlooked. Finding a smaller company that can benefit from your specialized attention is preferable. Smaller trucking companies benefit from mom-and-pop shops. Don't assume that just because they're small, they won't bring you much business. Even if you deal with a small company, it can provide you with 50 loads per month. Take a drive around the neighborhood and write down the names of the local industrial parks. Check out their businesses on Google, and you might be able to locate some stable work for the long term. Because most of these small companies are domestic, their loads may be located within the state or in neighboring states. You should also try focusing on seasonal businesses.

6.14 Start with a customer email or phone call

You must not get frustrated if you call a person and are responded to by a computerized answering machine. During your quest for your customers, you will have to deal with computers instead of real people. But you must not give up and should keep trying. Those computer voices are your potential customers. If you're lucky, you'll succeed in contacting the concerned person who could connect you with the shipping officer. This is simply fabulous because it means you'll get a real person to talk to rather than a generic "shippingoffice@business.com" email address. Persistence is required in achieving success. You must be aware of the contacts you're making. Are they interested or uninterested? It's your job to persuade them to talk to you. All you need to do is ask one simple question. "Are you having any shipping issues right now?" It is your responsibility to solve the problems of your customers. You must first understand their issues if you want to resolve them. So go ahead and ask them. "Can you tell me about your problem?"

- Do you need another quote?
- Is there a bad lane that you are having trouble with?
- Is your latest inventory stuck on the dock rather than on the road owing to the unavailability of another driver?

You can explain what you have in your first contact, such as how many trucks and trailers you have to support them in solving their problems. It isn't perfect, but it is effective.

Weekly contact with customers keeps your name in front of them

You'll have to send an email or make a phone call once a week. You should not anticipate an exponential rise in contract numbers. This is a long-term strategy. You must have a system in place that is effective for you. You could indeed send your first contact to a prospective customer via email or phone and wait a week before following up. A week later, you send another contact, informing them that you are in their area and ready to assist them. You'll do it again the following week, asking if there's a lane you could bid on. You could also extend your help in resolving their bad lane issue. You always make an effort to keep things optimistic and friendly.

Find the freight broker

One of the most popular ways of connecting truckers and shippers is through freight brokers. Because they do most of the work to match loads with drivers, they can save the owner-operators a lot of time and effort. Of course, they charge a fee for the service, so business owners should be aware of any additional costs. Furthermore, because brokers usually negotiate rates with shippers, the owner-operator will need to determine the profit potential of a particular load.

Negotiate a contract directly with the shipper

If you can negotiate a contract and enter into an agreement directly with a shipper for getting loads, you will save yourself from a lot of hassle. This will almost certainly necessitate cold calling. In other words, you'll need to contact shippers, get yourself introduced, and inquire about the possibility of a private contract. Calls take a little time and don't be surprised if the majority of the people you talk with do not respond positively. This is standard procedure for any cold calling. However, do your research and locate local shippers who may be looking for an exclusive driver. You will be better able to explain owner-operator load rates and succeed in creating perpetual revenue streams.

Become a government contractor

The local as well as state and federal governments have transportation requirements. Choosing to work as a government contractor is one way for owner-operators to find loads. To haul their load, you have first to get yourself registered as a government contractor instead of other types of loads. On the other hand, you can team up with another company that already has a government contract. If you're interested in executing government trucking contracts, you must also contact the state or city government for more information.

Use a truckload board

This is probably the simplest and most efficient, and effective way for truckers to find loads. Truckload boards' display tells you exactly what needs to be shipped, as well as where it is, where it is to be delivered, its exact weight, and any other job-specific information.

Owner-operators could indeed make a quick decision, provide the shipper with rates and other information, and be on their way. For decades, the trucking industry has leaned heavily on truckload boards. Truckload boards were once only observed at truck stops. However, the truck load boards have been digitized and available on your computer or mobile phone.

For owner-operators, carriers, and fleet managers, some of the many advantages of using advanced electronic truckload boards include:

- Owner-operators and fleet managers looking for loads can use truck load boards to expedite the process.
- They can often assist new owner-operators in getting the required truckloads in less time by matching truckloads to their location and equipment.
- Load boards could indeed reduce deadhead by letting owner-operators book their next load in the same area as their current destination
- A few load boards allow the owner-operators on the price negotiation process
- Load boards give drivers leeway in their driving and working schedule

6.15 How to scale your business?

If you own a small trucking company, you know how difficult it is to gain a competitive edge over large fleets. The obvious benefit of having more trucks is that they could offer more competitive rates, hire drivers faster, negotiate better supplier discounts, and generally capitalize on their size to deliver faster. So, it is a challenging task to grow amidst large companies with huge fleets in today's trucking and transportation industry. Things you can do right now to achieve sustainable growth are listed below:

Anticipate trucking industry regulations

Nothing stays the same in the trucking industry. The trucking industry's new regulations, amendments in existing regulations, and other proposed changes in the industry call for staying current on all matters. The year 2020 began with five new regulations which had a tremendous impact on the industry. It's still unclear what changes will take effect in 2021, as a new White House administration will undoubtedly leave its mark on transportation.

Democrats, on the whole, are more pro-regulation, particularly when it comes to environmental and safety regulations.

Keep up with transportation technology

Since you own the trucking company, you have to be responsible for executing multifarious tasks. It can be difficult to run a small business while you are on the road.

The best part is that technology could indeed assist you in becoming more organized, managing your finances, reducing stress, navigating the road, and much more. Use GPS, for example, to find the best routes and ways to integrate loads for cost savings.

You can save time and enhance your trucking company efficiency by using the apps. Listed below are some of the trucking apps that you can use right now for immediate impact:

Keep Trucking

It is the most popular app that has been built for drivers. It gives you violation alerts and helps you recap working hours. It also helps you to send logs via email.

Given below are some of its features:

- HOS alerts of upcoming required breaks
- Creation of electronic DVIRs
- Automated IFTA reporting

Trucker Tools

Given below are some of the striking features of this app:
- Real-time traffic info
- Turn-by-turn directions
- Keeps you current on the weigh-scale status
- Gives you accurate truck stops along your route
- Informs you of weather conditions
- You remain aware of the nearest diesel prices

Keep using Trucker Tools for saving money on the road.

Fuel book

It allows you to search diesel prices at more than 7,000 truck stops nationwide. This app helps the trucking community save on fuel over 21 million times.

6.16 Master your business finances

Therefore, since you are a trucker, you know where you've been, where you are, and where you're going as a trucker. However, as a trucking company owner, you must be aware of all of these factors in your finances. Consider the following scenario:

- Your major expense items
- Your current balances
- Your objectives, revenue expectations, and expenses

To help you accomplish your growth targets, you must quickly and efficiently create a business plan.

6.17 Commitment to providing the best service

It may appear simple, but this is one area where the big boys may be unable to compete with you.

Because you're a smaller business, you're more agile, hungry, and have fewer clients.

So, treat each one as if they were your most important client, and your phone will continue to ring. People today are still willing to pay a premium for the perks of a premium service. Relationships, not clients, will help you grow your trucking company.

6.18 Define plans for business growth

You should figure out the investment that you will need to pump in to accomplish your growth goals.

You should also be able to calculate the period that would be required for accomplishing your trucking company's expansion goals.

This approach will enable you to comprehend the complexities of growing a small fleet and thus help you achieve your targets.

6.19 Look for clients with load boards and freight brokers

Truckload boards, also known as freight boards, are an excellent way for trucking companies to locate available loads. Truckers and fleet owners can use the boards to look for criteria that match their qualifications with the types of loads they want to move. It's a fantastic way of building relations with shippers.

6.20 Be smart

As a self-employed truck driver, you must find loads that allow you to drive less while earning the same amount of money. Therefore, since you are an owner-operator, you must not think and work as a company driver. You must begin working smarter to increase your earnings. To accomplish this, you must avoid loads that require you to drive more deadhead miles. Because fewer miles are driven, less money is spent on fuel, your truck is less stressed, you spend less time working, and you make more money.

6.21 Manage your cash flow wisely

Freight bills are commonly not paid before delivery. Moreover, it is quite expensive to get the freight bills delivered.

If you're a large transportation company, that's fine, but if you're a small or midsize fleet, you'll often need immediate cash to fuel the trucks and pay your drivers. A third-party factor purchases your invoices for a small fee with freight invoicing, taking small fleets and owner-operators into account. They take over the collections or accounts receivable responsibilities, and you get paid sooner rather than later. Other cost-cutting benefits include the best fuel cards for the trucking company, reduced insurance rates, and truck leasing assistance. Freight factoring allows you to free up cash flow and gain faster access to working capital, allowing you to expand your business more quickly.

STARTUP BUSINESS

CHAPTER 7:

The Most Common Reasons Why Trucking Business Fails

The trucking industry is booming, and owner-operators have seen a steady increase in revenue over the last few years. Trucking companies can be massively lucrative, but only if you have a thorough understanding of the industry. Trucking companies, on the other hand, do fail. Knowing the main causes of their failure could help you avoid the same mistakes and point you in the right direction instead. It would help if you avoided the following mistakes as an owner-operator:

7.1 Poor management

Good employees are scared away by bad managers. Gallup, a research and advisory firm, discovered that one out of two employees quit their jobs because of a bad boss. According to Arcos Advisors, poor managers cost the economy a minimum of $319 billion per year. In the transportation business, personality differences aggravate the issue. Truck drivers, for example, often quit a business because they do not like the dispatcher or fleet manager. The majority of a driver's time has been spent on the road. They're patient, yet they can't take criticism well. They also require better structure.

On the contrary, managers lack guidance and try to thrive in an aggressive environment. It's difficult to find good, honest drivers, so losing them is a waste because of your fleet manager. Furthermore, there has been a driver shortage in the trucking industry. In 2018, the American Trucking Associations reported that the industry had a shortage of almost 60,800 drivers. By 2028, that number is expected to increase by at least 160,000 people. If you lose a driver, you might not be able to find a suitable replacement.

A trucking company's business would be greatly undermined without drivers. You won't be able to fill orders, which will put a strain on the other drivers. Consequently, they would be compelled to work longer hours to keep up with demand.

7.2 Bad managers make bad business decisions

Good leaders are not fool-proof from making poor business decisions. According to a Forbes article, force their plan and make decisions based on what they believe will help them advance.

Poor managers, on the other hand, make disastrous decisions.

They are disengaged from their employees and frequently lose sight of the big picture. The damage caused by bad managers, according to Small Business Chronicle, is extensive.

They not only scare away good talent, but they also make employees challenge senior management's support for a bad leader and fail to build relationships with their subordinates. Moreover, they demoralize the employees.

Their actions and decisions result in low performance, mismanagement of resources, and missing various business opportunities.

What you should do to avoid hiring a bad manager

The senior management should take the following steps if they want to avoid hiring a bad manager:

- Choose the right manager
- Define and communicate their expectations
- Get the managers educated and trained on the aspects of high performance

7.3 Poor management of finances

Smaller trucking companies are more vulnerable to poor financial management. However, this mistake is also made by larger companies.

Most trucking business owners have no idea what their business is worth or how much they would have to spend to earn profit.

You should be aware that not understanding your finances is a good way to start down the path to bankruptcy. Do you have any idea how profitable you'll be this year? Or do you simply hope that the revenues will cover all of your expenses and leave you with a profit margin?

Did you know that the average cost per mile for trucking companies is $1.69, according to the latest American Transportation Research Institute report?

This figure includes driver pay and benefits and vehicle-related expenses like fuel, lease and purchase payments, repair and maintenance, truck insurance premiums, permits and licenses, tires, and tolls. Your trucking company's operational costs will, of course, differ from the average. You should calculate your operational costs using the same cost considerations outlined above.

7.4 No clue of how much to charge for your services

No company can succeed by giving away its goods and services for free. It's the same if you start reducing your prices below the actual cost. After you've determined your own cost per mile, you'll need to determine how much to charge per mile. How do you figure out your prices?

- Select a freight lane. A freight lane is a route that is used for transporting goods.
- After defining your freight lane, you need to take a look at load boards. Find ten loads in your preferred freight lane going in one direction and see how much they pay.
- Calculate the average of these quotations.
- Charge the price that will cover your costs.

7.5 Violating rules and not minding compliance

You should be aware of and ensure compliance with regulations as a trucking company owner. That's because breaking these rules can cost you a lot of money, and in some cases, the US Department of Transportation may order you to close down your business. The Federal Motor Carrier Safety Administration, for example, has recently increased fines for breaking federal trucking regulations. The minimum fine for violations is more than $300 and can reach over $191,000 in some cases. The fines will be determined by the nature of the trucking business as well as the violation. The DOT may suspend you or order you to close your business if you refuse to listen. You'll be charged another $24,017 if you keep operating during the suspension.

7.6 Not getting help when you need it

Smaller trucking firms have a flat hierarchy. The owner also serves as a dispatcher, accountant, safety manager, and sales and marketing director. Small firms do not hire a lot of staff because of cost considerations. Therefore, they perform most of the tasks themselves. However, as your company grows, you may find yourself juggling too many things at once, which can lead to a lot of mistakes. You must hire competent and professional people for your trucking company. If you don't think you'll need full-time employees, you can hire professional services to handle certain aspects of your business. You can hire the services of an accountant for the management of your finances. You can also get in touch with a lawyer to deal with regulatory matters.

7.7 Problems with the economy or the industry

It's not always your fault. There are times when the industry you are working in goes through turmoil. The trucking industry had a difficult year in 2019. At least eight trucking companies had to shut down their businesses in the year 2019. Over 2,600 drivers were laid off as a result of the closures. However, going through a difficult period should not be used as an excuse. The things we've suggested above, such as properly planning your business, analyzing your cash flow, and understanding the basics of the trucking industry, will help you deal appropriately with all challenges.

7.8 Driver Shortage

What's the reason behind the downward trend? One of the reasons was trucking companies' failure in hiring more than 60,800 drivers. The issue is that, as some states legalize marijuana, trucking companies find it difficult to find drivers who can pass a drug test. Passing the drug test is one of the job requirements. In addition, fewer people are applying for the post. It's difficult to stay on the road for a long period.

7.9 Not meeting customer expectations correctly

There is a general misconception that the best way to attract customers is to offer the lowest price to them compared to your competitors. This scenario, however, is a losing scenario for both you and your competitors. If you don't make enough money, you won't maintain your vehicles or hire and retain excellent drivers. Furthermore, operations would be hampered over time. Rather than engaging in a price war with the competitors, you should focus on fulfilling your customers' requirements and needs.

On-time deliveries

The clients do not want an overabundance of stocks in their warehouse. This not only takes up too much space in the warehouse, but it also has an impact on the taxes they pay. The clients do not want their stocks lying on shelves. They prefer to have products delivered on demand. If trucking companies make on-time deliveries, they can assist them in achieving this goal.

Transport that is safe and secure

Clients want their orders to arrive in good condition. If you have to tell them that their goods have been lost or stolen in an accident, you are not providing the greatest customer care.

Reasonable rates

After analyzing the competitive environment, you should always try to offer reasonable rates for your service. This way, you will be able to grow and expand in a short period. It will also help you achieve your growth and profitability objectives.

7.10 Not investing in technology

The worst mistake that a trucking company can make is to remain indifferent to technology. New technological tools are often costly, but they do have some advantages for your company. ELDs and telemetric are examples of new technology that can help you automate and streamline logging and inspection.

Dynamic routing

On a typical day, you're transporting goods and people from one location to another. Your deliveries arrive sooner, and your drivers avoid getting stuck in traffic jams. Dynamic routing aids in the discovery of the most efficient routes. It can also make the most efficient trip planning possible. Your drivers will be able to save money on gas and time on the road due to this.

Driver scorecards

These technologies will assist you in determining how well your drivers perform while on the road. Driver scorecards will keep an eye out for bad driving habits, calculate the miles per gallon, and assign a score to your drivers. This will allow you to determine which drivers require additional training.

Technologies that help in avoiding accidents

There are now devices with sensors that can detect when you are about to collide with something and avoid the collision.

For example, the Wingman Fusion utilizes video and radar to track the vehicles and the road ahead. It also includes an electronic stability program to aid your drivers in avoiding loss of control.

Trailer Trackers

GPS technology can assist you in keeping track of your truck's location. Fleet managers can use trailer trackers to track down a stolen trailer. Trailer trackers can also warn the drivers if they are driving through an area where theft is common.

7.11 Choosing the wrong people as partners

Business partnerships can ruin friendships, so try to avoid them. If you must form a partnership, ensure you have an operating agreement in place, as well as fully documented business documents and an exit strategy.

7.12 Not knowing the real cost per mile

The majority of customer quotes are based on cost per mile. The concept behind the calculation is straightforward: figure out your cost per mile and charge more than that. Undoubtedly calculating your fuel costs and driver pay/mile is incredibly easy, but are you aware of your insurance, maintenance, IFTA, tolls, etc. Due to their ignorance of various key cost figures, the owner-operators compute the cost per mile based on incomplete information.

CHAPTER 8:

The Pros and Cons of a Trucking Business

Listed below are the pros and cons of the trucking business.

8.1 Pros of trucking business

Listed below are the pros of the trucking business.

An easy start

It doesn't take years of education or a lot of training or experience to get into trucking. When you're ready, all you have to do is get a commercial driver's license (CDL) and take a quick course to learn the basics. Whether you require immediate employment or despise the prospect of returning to school, trucking makes launching a career simply.

Job security

Truckers are in high demand, and that is unlikely to change anytime soon. According to a reliable source, approximately three-quarters of freight tonnage reaches its destination with the help of the trucking industry. In the absence of the trucking industry, the entire retail business would come to a sudden end. Truckers will have absolute job security as a result of this. You can work as a truck driver for as long as you want. However, you should have your own CDL as well as a good driving record. You could indeed move across the country or abandon a company you don't like without fear of losing your job — something that isn't true in most industries.

An independent workday

When you work as a truck driver, you don't have to worry about being distracted by coworkers or having a boss looking over your shoulder all day. Truckers have the unique advantage of operating independently. Moreover, the truckers have their schedules.

You have complete control over when you want to take breaks, the type of music you can enjoy while driving, and your work-dress.

Decision making

Compared to working for a large trucking company, owner-operators have more freedom to choose what loads to haul. They also are free to choose their clients and decide on their work schedule. The ability to make the above decisions carries numerous benefits and can help keep owner-operators in control.

Profitability

The owner-operators enjoy a major portion of the profit from their loads. They also generate more revenue than truck drivers working for a company. Owner-operators control every aspect of truck driving responsibility and thus collect the profit by owning the truck, setting up the shipment contract, and delivering the goods.

8.2 Cons of the trucking business

Listed below are the cons of the trucking business.

Time

Think again if you believe you are working full time for a large trucking company as a dispatcher. Because they have a much larger workload to cover on their own, owner-operators work even harder than company truck drivers.

Owner-operators don't have much downtime between maintaining the truck, setting up contracts, and hauling the freight.

Responsibility

Owning a business gives you confidence and teaches commitment in your approach towards managing the various affairs of the business. At the same time, it calls for accepting responsibility for any mistakes you make. If they want to run a successful trucking business, owner-operators must always be top of their work. They also need to remain aware of government regulations.

Stress

Starting as an owner-operator can be very stressful until establishing a distinctive and unique reputation in the industry. This is substantiated if you start receiving loads regularly. Owner-operators must constantly network and build their brand as a credible source for hauling freight on top of needing the funding to run their operation.

Startup Costs

Starting a trucking company, like starting any other business, can be expensive. However, there are financing options available, particularly for startups in the transportation industry. So, while it can be costly, there are ways for you to be your boss.

Consider freight bill factoring to get cash flowing in right away if you've considered the pros and cons and still want to be an owner-operator. Even if you're just starting and don't have any business credit, freight factoring companies can provide instant funding on freight bills. By factoring in freight costs, owner-operators may obtain the financing to carry more cargoes and improve profitability without depending on client payment.

The potential for an unhealthy lifestyle

Spending an entire day on the road restricts the food options for truck drivers. When you see a McDonald's sign, it's easy and tempting to pull off the highway. However, a lot of junk food and soft drinks are not good for your health in the long term. You need to practice healthy eating habits. That is something that truckers must remember. They should focus on nutritious items and bring healthy snacks with them on the road.

8.3 Secrets and tips to increase profit and have a successful trucking business

The trucking industry has a lot of potentials. While technology is leading the way, if you want to succeed in the highly competitive industry, you must know the following secrets of the trucking business.

Instant information

Good decisions mean better business in any industry. The success of a business is influenced by the quality of the good decisions along with their timely implementation. One bad decision can have a huge impact on the entire company. Thus for making decisions that impact funding and progress necessitates detailed and current information. A lack of critical information can influence even micro-decisions like resource assignment on total outstanding orders. It would help if you had custom software to run a successful trucking business because it instantaneously displays all critical business information on the screen. You should be able to select which specific information should be displayed automatically while using this software.

- Accounts receivable
- Accounts payable
- Owner-operator liability
- Outstanding orders
- Credit lines
- Net profits and so on

Total information integration

Lack of inter-branch coordination about sharing critical information could pave the way for bottlenecks, resulting in irritated employees, irritated drivers, lost packages, and dissatisfied customers, not to mention the loss of millions of dollars. A fully integrated software for the trucking business helps achieve synergy. You can record and update your trucking orders, view your bills, charges, generate invoices and monitor the entire process quite easily on a single screen. Real-time transaction processing instantly updates all related data, ensuring that you have the most up-to-date information.

Customer satisfaction

Finding customers willing to pay for your goods or services is difficult, but keeping them is even more difficult. There are two types of customers in the trucking industry: those who seek the lowest prices and those who prefer excellent service even if it means paying a higher price. Trying to attract more customers by offering the lowest prices is a losing battle because you will have to sacrifice the service quality. If you don't have enough cash flow, you won't hire good drivers or maintain safe, well-maintained equipment. You pay low wages to truckers who then leave for better-paying jobs, and your trucks break down due to poor maintenance. Paying and treating truck drivers well will result in better results, happier customers, and a better reputation. Customer satisfaction is ensured through appropriate rates, safe transportation, and timely delivery.

Happy truckers

Talented employees who are aligned with a company's business goals are critical to its success. You must put time and effort into finding the right people, whether office staff to handle logistics or truck drivers/mechanics. Even if you successfully hire the best employees, you must also learn to keep them and increase their productivity. Keeping your truck drivers satisfied is a long-term business strategy that pays off. Without trucks, there is no trucking business. Similarly, you cannot run your trucking business without the help of drivers. You must realize that the key to a trucking company's success has efficient and productive truck drivers.

Quick and accurate settlements

Getting your truck drivers' paychecks on time is one thing that guarantees a big smile on their faces. However, you might be surprised to learn that many good drivers leave the company after years of fighting with the accounting department on various payment issues. The key to a successful trucking company is to ensure that all payments are made on time and without causing any problems for the parties involved. You'll need the right tools to generate accurate and simple driver settlements based on pay rates and hours worked, miles driven, advances, charge-backs, and other factors. Default pay rates could be set by revenue percentages or hourly rates, allowing the system to automatically calculate the driver's pay from the order. The payment is credited to the driver's account once the order is completed. Losing professional drivers could indeed cost you a lot of money in terms of money and time spent on recruiting, training, and lost business.

Visual dispatch system

Truck dispatchers are the trucking industry's backbone. These are the people who work behind the scenes to ensure that truck drivers have their cargo. Moreover, they assist them in concentrating on the best routes to their destination, adhering to their scheduled arrival times, and safely delivering their loads. Poor customer intelligence and outdated order management tools stifle their productivity, resulting in deferred revenue orders and lost loads. Equip your dispatchers with Real-time Visual Dispatching systems that give them full access to the data needed to make quick decisions when it matters. They should move seamlessly from the order screen to the dispatch screen and assign equipment and drivers with a single click.

Constant cash flow

A steady cash flow is necessary to keep a trucking company alive and running. Even if the trucking company is good and your income and expense statements appear to be in order, cash flow issues can cause your company to falter and eventually fail. When the majority of the profit is locked up in receivables, then you are bound to fail. When companies don't have the time or workforce to chase down outstanding receivables, billing times and outstanding receivables arise. The first step toward improving your cash flow is to eliminate order processing errors. It's critical to implement the appropriate software to help reduce errors and the time it takes to process sales and manage expenses. You should also try to shorten when your service is delivered and when you are paid for it.

Automated IFTA reports

Streamlining your trucking company's administration and record-keeping can be a difficult and time-consuming task. Because handwritten driver reports and related receipts must be collected and interpreted, manually processing all of the information required to create the report consumes a lot of time. Some businesses even hire freelancers to handle IFTA tax returns. Implementing user-friendly telematics solutions to monitor and manage mobile assets and employees is a better option.

Intuitive tracking solutions

The fleet management solutions could indeed help you save money while increasing efficiency. If you're considering starting a trucking company, or if you already have one but want to expand, getting a great trucking software solution could indeed help you a lot in accomplishing your growth objectives. A good trucking software solution, developed by someone who understands the industry's needs, will include the following features

- managing and dispatching shipments
- real-time tracking
- freight bid management

Book 2:

Freight Broker

Introduction

Of course, in an ideal world, each entity in the business would perform its day-to-day function, and that's all. However, the transportation sector is evolving at such a fast pace that once-clear boundaries are constantly blurring. A successful freight broker may also grow their company by forming subsidiaries or other businesses that provide additional freight services. This book will teach you all you need to know about freight brokers.

Brokers are not new to the trucking business; they have existed since the industry's inception in the early twentieth century. Before the 1970s, however, broker rules were so stringent that few companies were even ready to attempt to get into the sector. Regulatory restrictions have relaxed due to significant changes in the federal transportation policy throughout the 1970s, providing new entrepreneurial possibilities in the third-party logistics provider sector. A freight broker acts as a go-between for shippers and carriers. The broker enables contact between the carrier and the shipper rather than taking possession of the freight. They're in charge of ensuring that the handoff between shippers and carriers happens well and that freight reaches safely and on schedule. Shippers like to deal with freight brokers as they have just a single point of contact from start to end as their freight travels to its final destination. Dealing with a carrier, arranging routes, and monitoring freight are all made easier when working with a broker. Carriers also like collaborating with freight brokers to improve their routes and reduce deadhead miles, allowing them to make more money in less time. Freight brokers utilize their knowledge to reduce delivery times, minimize damage, and enhance the efficiency of your supply chain. These brokers provide lower prices because they pool the freight volume of all the shippers with whom they do business, allowing them to negotiate lower rates that they pass on to the clients.

CHAPTER 1:

Responsibilities of freight broker

A freight broker is a middleman that connects two businesses by locating, evaluating, and commissioning a motor carrier that transports products for a shipper. The freight broker makes certain that the products reach safely at their ultimate destination. They profit by taking the difference between the amount paid by the shipper and the amount accepted by the motor carrier as payment. A freight broker facilitates the shipment of products by acting as a middleman between shippers and carriers. Customers are matched with freight carriers, orders are booked, and carriers are lined up for loading by freight brokers. Freight delivery broker is another name for it. Both motor shippers and carriers benefit from the services provided by brokers. In return for a commission, they help carriers in filling their vehicles. Several businesses utilize brokers as their traffic department, enabling them to handle all of their transportation and shipping management requirements via the broker. You may become a freight broker in one of two ways: an independent broker or an employee of a brokerage company. An independent freight broker deals with their contracts with shipping companies and is paid directly by them.

A freight broker's typical responsibilities include:

- Creating sales leads for the business
- Creating sales leads for the business
- Locating, vetting, and commissioning a carrier to transport commodities
- Tracking, controlling, and informing the shipper about the items' journey
- Managing and resolving unforeseen circumstances that occur during the transportation of products
- Completing the delivery procedure

- Creating a sales pipeline, as well as generating leads and recruiting new prospects.
- Identifying and choosing trustworthy and safe freight carriers.
- Providing shipping quotations to clients.
- Making reservations with carriers.
- Assisting with the loading of carriers.
- Monitoring the status of loads.
- Working with carriers, shippers, and dispatchers to coordinate planned pickups and deliveries.
- Keeping detailed records of all relevant actions.
- Keeping clients up to date on shipping progress and helping with any questions.
- Keeping up to date on market developments in the transportation industry.

STARTUP BUSINESS

CHAPTER 2:

Licensing and business registration

Before starting the application process to become a freight broker, candidates need to understand what a freight broker is. In a nutshell, a freight broker serves as a connection between a business that needs products shipment and an authorized motor carrier.

Although freight brokers do not carry products, they collect information about the business's needs and connect them with a carrier that can convey those items for a fair price. Some candidates choose to participate in broker training programs before applying for their license to understand a freight broker better.

You will need a freight broker license, also known as a load broker license, if you wish to operate as a freight broker, connecting products that must be transported with trucking firms that perform the shipment.

The Federal Motor Carrier Safety Administration (FMCSA) regulates freight brokers, and the rules may be complicated.

Fortunately, following a step-by-step procedure is all you need to do. So, how can you obtain your license as a freight broker? Here's everything you need to know.

2.1 Establish a Business Structure

An applicant's first step in getting licensed is to figure out how they want their business to be organized. When making this choice, it is strongly recommended that you speak with an attorney or accountant, as they will balance the benefits and drawbacks of various company forms with the licensee. Whether or not a consultation is required, an applicant must finally choose one of the following three formats for their freight broker license:

- Individual/Sole Proprietor
- Corporation
- Partnership

2.2 Submit an OP-1 Form

After establishing your company structure, you will need to apply for a motor carrier number by submitting a completed OP-1 form to the FMCSA. This is the first application form that applicants send to the FMCSA, and it contains basic business information (name, type of operating authority, company type, address, etc.) Applicants should choose "Broker of Property" or "Broker of Household Goods" (excluding Household Goods) in Section III of the OP-1 form for Type of Operating Authority. In addition, applicants must pay a $300 application fee for each kind of license they seek.

If you apply for a motor carrier number online, you will get it right away, while those who apply by mail may have to wait up to four weeks. The motor carrier number is needed to go forward with the freight broker licensing procedure, and it gives the company formal permission to operate. The motor carrier number is subject to a 10-day objection process once it is granted. During this period, another business may challenge the application. During the protest period, the applicant may continue the process of acquiring a freight broker license.

2.3 Get a Surety Bond (BMC-84)

The surety bond requirement is frequently the most challenging of all the stages in the licensing process. Many applicants have never heard of surety bonds until discovering that they are required to get a license. Furthermore, the federal freight broker bond is more difficult to acquire than other kinds of bonds. Because the freight brokerage business has a greater level of risk, acceptance for the bond is based on the particular applicant's history, among other things.

Despite the widespread misconceptions about surety bonds, they are simple contracts used in various sectors to guarantee that the company that secures the bond—the principal—conducts business according to all applicable laws and regulations. The obligee is the person that requests the bond and has the right to sue if the principal fails to follow the bond's terms and conditions. The surety is the third party in the arrangement, and they are the ones who issue the bond once the principal pays them a premium. The premium is a proportion of the total bond amount that the surety promises to pay the obligee if there is a claim. If a lawsuit is made and the surety pays money to resolve the claim, the principal—in this instance, the freight broker—is responsible for reimbursing the surety for the money paid to settle the claim.

Before July 2012, individuals seeking freight broker licenses were needed to acquire a $10,000 surety bond. The adoption of the Moving Ahead for Progress in the Twenty-First Century Act (MAP-21) in October 2013 raised the bond amount needed of freight brokers to $75,000. The rise was prompted by the high number of claims filed against these bonds due to principle misbehavior, ensuring that only competent candidates were granted a freight broker license.

Because freight broker bonds are credit-based and subject to underwriting, applicants must provide financial information when applying. Please visit our dedicated bond page for more information on the BMC-84 freight broker surety bond, which focuses only on the freight broker bond, how costs are calculated, and what you may anticipate spending.

Unlike freight forwarders and motor carriers, the FMCSA does not require freight brokers to have insurance beyond a surety bond, but some customers may want to see evidence of insurance before doing business with them.

2.4 Select a Process Agent

A representative upon whom the court documents may be served in any action filed against a broker, motor carrier, or freight forwarder, according to the FMCSA.

Every registered freight broker must designate a process agent in each state where it has an office and executes contracts to comply with 49 CFR 366. Freight brokers may designate several process agents or engage with a firm that provides blanket coverage after obtaining their motor carrier number. This coverage enables a single individual to serve as a process server in several states. Irrespective of how many process agents are chosen, the freight broker or authorized process agent must complete and submit Form BOC-3 to the FMCSA on behalf of the freight broker.

2.5 Register the Brokerage

All freight brokers must participate in the Unified Carrier Registration as the last stage in the licensing procedure. This is the agreement created as part of the Unified Carrier Registration Plan that governs the collecting and distribution of financial responsibility information and registration supplied by brokers, as well as the fees they pay. It sets regulations and laws for all freight brokers, including fees to be paid to the freight broker's base-state or the state where their primary office is situated.

Brokers must acquaint themselves with local laws involving interstate businesses for each state in which they will be doing business by consulting the state's transportation regulatory agency, in addition to participating in the Unified Carrier Registration.

2.6 What to Do After Getting a License

After the FMCSA issues, the license, and the registration are finished, the licensee may start doing business as a freight broker. They may, however, be unsure about where to begin.

Run the Business

The majority of freight broker business is conducted over the phone and through email. Establish an office with a dedicated phone line, a computer, and high-speed internet access. Begin by establishing your freight carriers.

For air, rail, and truck transportation services, you will need dependable connections. Once you have established those relationships and procedures for booking freight, it is time to locate clients and begin scheduling shipments.

This is a difficult phase that requires sales abilities. Establish your target audiences, create call lists, and begin calling. Go to the carriers and price the shipments when you have a customer ready to send freight. Send the customer your price together with your internal markup. If they agree, go on to contracts and shipping dates.

Make an effort to convert your regular shippers into long-term clients. Repeat business cuts down on the amount of time you spend selling and improves your shipping load, boosting your earnings.

CHAPTER 3:

How important is knowing your target market

To be successful with any kind of marketing, whether conventional mailers and inbound marketing or cold calls, you must first understand your target audience. Identifying your target market audience is usually done at the planning stage of a company's development. One of the numerous questions you ask yourself while creating a product or service is, "Who do I want to appeal to the most?" or "Who is this going to appeal to?"

These inquiries are critical to the development of your marketing plan. If you develop a novel method for removing wrinkles from clothes, you may attract a wide range of customers. The product may be beneficial to homemakers since it saves them time and money. It may be useful for travelers, particularly business people, to keep their clothes appearing fresh after they have been packed away. Anyone who has wrinkled clothes or material that needs to be straightened may benefit from the product. You may attempt to reach out to all of these groups, or you could concentrate on a smaller group that you think would be a better starting point and then expand it later.

3.1 Knowing your target market is important, but you also need buyer personas in today's digital world.

Knowing who your target audience is can help you decide which marketing techniques to use. A lot of blogs exist that provide information to assist companies in engaging their target audience. If the business chose to concentrate on the homemakers in the example above, a content marketing strategy and blogging would be a fantastic place to start. Offering advice on how to clean effectively around the house and focusing on the keyword phrases "saving money" or "cleaning tips" may help the blog show up in fairly frequent search queries within their audience. Including articles about their product that contain the primary keywords and more targeted ones like "how to repair wrinkled clothing" or "how to remove wrinkles without an iron" may help them attract more visitors and business. This is often accomplished by using inbound marketing strategies.

The fundamental elements required to create a successful marketing campaign include having a clear concept of the audience you want to target and to whom your product or service might be most helpful. Identify the words that your consumers may use to describe the issue that your product or service solves, then go after those phrases aggressively via your website's content.

3.2 Inbound marketing success also requires adaptability.

It is still essential to be flexible and have a well-designed and appealing website and relevant content. The emphasis of content strategy and keyword marketing should change to the value and usefulness of the product or service at such time rather than anything else. The same is true when new trends emerge, threatening to render your products outdated or unpopular.

No business can just launch an inbound marketing strategy and call it a day. Maintaining your material adaptability to changes takes a lot of adjusting and fine-tuning, and staying on top of consumer trends. Thorough knowledge of your target market and customers is the foundation of any effective inbound marketing strategy.

When you switch to HubSpot CRM, you will get actionable insights from your contact database. You will also get access to a team of professionals that will do the grunt work for you. ManoByte's staff specializes in MarTech solutions for Building Materials Manufacturers, allowing you to increase sales via both direct and indirect channels.

CHAPTER 4:

Effective Business plan

Trucking is a well-established sector, and with the growing demand for outstation products, it may be very profitable. You may make trucking your main source of income if you put in the necessary effort and expertise. However, to thrive in business, you must first create a good business strategy. The trucking industry is very competitive, and a business plan may offer you the competitive advantage you need to survive and flourish. Continue reading to learn how.

A business strategy may assist you in putting things into perspective. It may offer you a clear picture of the industry's present state and where your company strategy could fit in. It also helps in formulating sound business plans and understanding what your rivals are up to. A solid business plan can assist you in figuring out which methods work and which don't. Furthermore, as a trucking company, a well-written business plan can assist you in running your business more smoothly and efficiently, with fewer issues, than a business that operates without a strategy and is all over the place.

Starting a freight brokerage company necessitates understanding how to perform the ideal function in assisting customers in filling their trucks and assisting shippers in finding dependable carriers. The freight brokerage industry dates back to the early twentieth century, and it is governed by government rules that have grown less stringent over time.

4.1 Outline of a Freight Trucking Business Plan

This is a typical freight trucking business model/plan outline that will cover all of the key parts that should be included in your plan.

- **Executive Summary**
  - Overview of the Company
  - Goals
  - Mission
  - Management Group
  - Success factors
  - Financial Overview (Year-by-Year Financial Highlights)

- **Company**
  - About GLTC
  1. Company Overview
  2. Company Summary
  - Management group
  - Hiring strategy

- **Products and Services**
  - Solution
  - Services and features

- **Competitive Analysis**
  - SWOT Analysis
  - Competitors

- **Target Market**
  - Market Overview
    1. Manufacturers
    2. Raw Material Suppliers
    3. Distributors or wholesalers
  - Market requirements
  - Industry Analysis

- **Financial Strategy**
  - Personnel Plan
  - Sales
  - Budget
  - Initial Investment
  - Cash Flow Predictions
  - Investments and loans

- **Financial Statements**
  - Profits and Losses Statement
  - Financial Statements
  - Statement of Cash Flows

CHAPTER 5:

Marketing and finding clients

Whether you are a truck driver looking for a break from long hours of driving or are new to shipping and eager to learn a new business, freight brokering is an interesting career choice within the trucking industry. A freight broker is a middleman who connects a shipper with goods to transport and a carrier with the required capacity to deliver them. The broker arranges transport, monitors the cargo, keeps track of shipments and pickups, and keeps the shipper up to date on the shipment status.

While some shippers have agreements with trucking firms to deliver their products, they may also deal with truck brokers. Brokers assist them in locating reputable carriers with a strong reputation and a track record of reliably transporting freight. They save time by not having to locate a carrier on their own, and the freight broker profits by paying the carrier less than the shipper is prepared to pay for their products to be transported.

5.1 Marketing

Technological advancements in transportation, logistics, and freight brokerage keep the logistics sector influx every year. Not only may these developments affect your freight management operations, but they can also affect how you advertise your business. Here are some of the most underutilized yet powerful freight agency marketing strategies.

1. Promote Your Niche

You may become a neighborhood hero for your local businesses if you have a distinct specialty. Promoting your niche to a larger audience may provide incredible results. Take your niche to a national or international level. You may be amazed at how many companies are searching for someone like you.

2. Advertise Your Freight business to Other Companies

It is easy to become stuck searching for leads in the same areas over and over again. However, go outside the usual freight pool of prospective shippers and find different companies that may benefit from your services. You may be able to tap into a hitherto undiscovered pool of customers.

If you reside in a city where specialized companies or small startups are transporting their goods, advertise freight management services to them. You may provide introductory rates to new businesses that might benefit from a shipping break. Not only will you be able to demonstrate to your community how you are assisting new companies in your neighborhood, but your new clients will also become the greatest supporters in your local market.

3. Utilize the Services of Professional Marketers to Promote Your Services

Your business is moving freight and logistics. To promote your business effectively, marketing does not have to be your strong point. Too many freight agents attempt to save money by performing the bare minimum or underestimating the value of freight agency marketing. To assist you in advertising your freight management services, choose a reputable marketing company specializing in logistics. Investing in experts who can create a successful marketing strategy for you will pay off and enable you to remain focused on your primary business – moving freight – unless you are prepared to put in the work required to do it yourself.

4. Loyalty should be rewarded with promotional giveaways.

It is one thing to advertise to increase lead generation. You want to keep those leads coming back after you have turned them into customers. Of course, providing excellent service is the most effective method to do this. However, you may enhance client loyalty by rewarding them with special freebies and discounts.

5. Encourage Referrals

In a similar vein, recommendations are the most powerful marketing instrument on the planet. The most successful method of freight agent marketing is still word-of-mouth. Encourage referrals on your website to create that sort of important word-of-mouth. Your clients will gladly help you if you perform a good job.

6. Offer delivery guarantees or price matching.

It is not always possible to provide freight delivery assurances. There may be instances when you cannot prevent delays. However, if you have a strong transportation carrier system and can confidently handle on-time deliveries despite road closures, bad weather, or other logistical difficulties, you may attract a lot of additional business by advertising that assurance.

If assurances, on the other hand, seem too risky, you might provide something equally beneficial - price matching. You will get notice if you give your clients competitive prices for freight management services. Your marketing efforts will be much more successful if you can match a smaller company's pricing or claim to beat your competitors' rates.

7. Engage with Your Clients and Customers

Finally, too many marketing plans, especially for freight brokers, overlook the value of client interaction as a marketing tool. You offer your consumers a feeling of friendship and familiarity that fosters loyalty when you react promptly to customer problems, engage in online conversations on your website, and truly seek feedback.

5.2 Finding clients

If you know how to attract the appropriate customers, going through freight broker training and becoming a registered broker may be a lucrative career move. As a truck broker, you have the potential to earn a lot of money, but only if you understand which shipments to target and how to manage the business side of things. Knowing what prospective clients are searching for is one of the keys to operating a successful business. A fair amount of effort and commitment is required to establish, maintain, and expand your client base. The steps in the following advice will assist you in identifying and contacting prospective customers.

1. Investigating Your Competitors

In addition to investigating prospective customers, you should also gather information on any potential rivals in your region. This may help you figure out whether there's a particular niche that needs to be filled or if some sectors have an excess of shipping choices. Examining the shipping alternatives utilized by companies in the same industry as your client's, or freight brokers with whom the customer has previously dealt, are excellent places to start. If you're researching businesses in your client's sector, check if you can learn how they transport their goods. This will offer you a behind-the-scenes look at the local freight brokerage alternatives and assist you in determining the best measures to take to be ahead of the competition. Examining your prospective client's unsuccessful working relationships with previous freight brokers is also beneficial. Why aren't they still utilizing that firm? How did the prior broker let the customer down? You will be able to avoid your competitors' faults and better meet your customers' needs if you learn from their missteps.

2. Examine your purchase history as well as those of previous customers.

Your records are another excellent source of information for possible leads. Consider the fact that every item you have bought has been transported, either from the manufacturer to the shop, the warehouse, or straight to you. Going through your purchasing history may help you spot prospective brokerage contracts in sectors you already know about, resulting in better client connections and a larger customer base.

Take a look at your shipping invoices and receipts for details. Where are the goods delivered to a foreign country? If so, how did it enter the country: via aircraft, truck, boat, or other means? Did the goods travel to a distribution center if it wasn't delivered straight to your home? What happened to this product before it arrived at its ultimate destination? All of these inquiries may lead to new customers or, at the very least, provide a starting point for your investigation. It is also a good idea to get feedback from previous consumers. You may identify and fix weaknesses in your brokerage approach and proactively avoid problems with future customers by evaluating why this person is no longer working with you. Alternatively, if customers no longer need your services due to a career move, you may re-establish your connection with a new contact within the business.

3. Cold Calling

Cold calling is a wonderful method to engage with prospective customers– and shippers. Because emails are easy to overlook or forget, a simple business call is frequently the most efficient way to contact and get the information you have to get started with a new customer. While some may argue that cold-calling companies with a sales presentation are too impersonal for effective relationship development, you should still have a plan in place for when you approach a new prospective customer. Make sure to provide a short description of your company, objectives, and how your experience pertains to this contract. Cold contacting your clients to inquire about their company demands and shipping demand for services is also a good way to do customer research.

Warm calling, similar to cold calling but needs a little more study, is another option. Before making a cold call, you should have a basic understanding of the shippers in your region and what services they may need. Although it takes more time to prepare, this method may help you build a working connection fast and effectively.

4. Using Calling Leads and Shipper Lists

You may also expand your company by using industry information such as shipper and manufacturer listings. There are many listings online, including MacRae's Blue Book website, which has a lot of information on shipping, production, and distribution firms. This site can tell you about prospective customers' location, company kind, product catalog— and, most crucially, their contact information. You may use shipper lists to limit down your customer search depending on your company requirements. Consider the case when you are acquainted with a certain product or can only travel to and from specific places. In such a scenario, you may search via a shipper list to identify the appropriate kind of prospective customers.

Using competition research, previous purchase data, and shipper lists may provide you with many customer possibilities. It is time to start contacting leads after you have gathered all the necessary information and written your short phone introduction. As previously said, phone calls are the most direct method to contact new business connections, thus utilizing your research to compile a list of leads to call may be a highly efficient way to discover new opportunities.

5. Using Search Engines

If you have exhausted all of your other research alternatives and are still looking for shippers, utilizing internet search engines is a fantastic method to do it. Google will almost certainly supply you with the basic information you need about virtually any big corporation as well as many small companies. A simple search will reveal the kinds of clients you're searching for, as well as their goods and, ideally, contact information.

Search engines may also help you find some unusual ways to find the ideal customers for your company. In many instances, Google offers a street-view or satellite option that allows you to learn more about a business before making contact. Based on the pictures, you may be able to determine whether the company has a big loading dock, a parking lot, or alleyway access that is too small for semi-trucks.

A freight broker may evaluate if they can successfully assist a shipper by examining all of the info that search engines offer. This will save you time by just contacting clients you already know can cooperate with your company.

CHAPTER 6:

How to become a successful freight broker and grow your business

Many individuals believe that establishing your freight brokerage is a simple and profitable method to succeed in the business. While there are many advantages to being a freight broker, there are also several dangers and expenses to consider before deciding whether it's the appropriate career path for you. Keep in mind that although the basic stages to become a freight broker are straightforward, being a successful freight broker is more difficult because many individuals overlook the difficulties before entering the profession. Freight brokerage has one of the greatest turnover rates of any industry, with many brokers quitting within the first year of operation. That's why we've put together this guide to assist you in becoming one of the third freight brokers who succeed in the long run. Licensed freight brokers work in a variety of areas throughout the globe, assisting clients with freight transportation. Over 17,000 freight brokers are operating in the United States today, either as sole proprietors or as part of a team. However, not every freight broker achieves the same level of success in their field. The following approaches are required to be a successful broker.

6.1 Acquire industry experience

Gaining the required expertise in the logistics or transportation sector is the first step toward a good career as a freight broker. Shippers and carriers are connected through freight brokers, who ensure that loads are delivered successfully and on time, and within budget.

Some freight brokers acquire this expertise by working for a trucking firm or truck driver, whereas others have worked in logistics positions for small and big businesses. This on-the-job training is an important part of learning what it takes to be a successful freight broker over time.

6.2 Recognize the Business Costs

Even though the costs of starting a freight brokerage company are cheap in comparison to other sectors, there are still expenditures to consider before becoming a broker. For commercial operations, freight brokers will likely require a computer and a specialized mobile phone, as well as technologies that assist expedite loading and link consumers to the process.

When combined with the license requirements listed below, these costs may total anything from a few hundred to - thousand dollars.

Understanding these expenses is essential for a broker to be ready to start and run a business.

6.3 Meet with the Licensing Requirements

To comply with federal laws and regulations, all freight brokers operating in the US must have a valid license. The Federal Motor Carrier Safety Administration, or FMCSA, levies a one-time cost for freight broker registration, which must be completed before dealing with any clients.

As part of business requirements, freight brokers must also acquire a bond or trust.

Failure to comply with these licensing criteria may have serious consequences for a freight broker, including the difficulty of getting a bond or license in the future.

6.4 Understanding the Differences Between a Trust and a bond

A trust or bond in the amount of $75,000 is one of the licensing criteria for becoming a freight broker. This obligation safeguards the broker's clients if business transactions do not adhere to federal regulations. The trust or the bond covers claims against a broker's company, which may be expensive for the broker. Because the cost of a freight broker bond is determined as a percentage of the overall bond need, it is the most popular option. A bond costs far less than a trust, which needs a broker to deposit the full $75,000 into a trust account upfront. Understanding these distinctions may help freight brokers save money both upfront and over time, enabling them to concentrate on other business needs and costs.

6.5 Build the Business Relationships

No freight broker can be successful until they have worked hard to develop long-term business connections.

Some business relationships are made via networking with other people in the transportation sector, while others are made through past employment or employers.

6.6 Have a Communication System

Productive freight brokers also have effective communication mechanisms in place, not just with prospects and clients but also with business connections. From phone and email conversations to texting and messaging apps, communication methods come in various forms. Successful brokers ensure that they constantly communicate useful and timely information with clients and business partners, regardless of the communication channel they employ.

6.7 Marketing the Business

Successful freight brokers recognize that the business is competitive, with more licensed brokers anticipated to join the market each year. As a result, brokers must develop a marketing plan for their businesses.

To encourage new clients to engage with the brokerage, marketing activities might include a social media message strategy, an email campaign, or radio or print advertising.

Some freight brokers attend local events or participate in online forums to network with shippers and carriers to expand their business reach.

6.8 Put in Effort and Time

Finally, if freight brokers are to achieve any level of success, they must be committed to the business. Brokers have the option of working as much or as little as they wish, but they best commit to a full work week to guarantee that their client's requirements are met daily.

6.9 Gain an understanding of the market

Analyzing and comprehending the market is the basic thing freight broker must do to succeed in their business. Only by doing so will you be aware of current logistics trends, what your rivals are up to, and what plans to devise to attract more leads.

The basic step in getting consumers to interact with your logistics firm is to have good communication. As a result, you should have a staff with extensive freight forwarding expertise and an understanding of what the target audience is searching for, and the ability to communicate effectively with them.

6.10 Invest into your differentials

Perhaps most significantly, a successful freight business will most likely increase revenues if they understand and operate around their differentials. That is, if you want the logistics business to stand out, you must ensure that you are correctly informing your prospects on the advantages they will get by choosing your services.

For example, if you're a smaller freight company, focus on providing a more personal and intimate level of service to your customers. Compared to bigger freight companies who cannot offer such a personal connection with their clients, this will provide your firm advantage.

CHAPTER 7:

How to find carriers and shippers

Freight brokers must understand consumer goods to locate shippers. What company makes them? What are their origins? What is the total number of goods they sell? These are the kind of inquiries you should make if you want to learn how freight brokers locate shippers.

7.1 The Leads Surround You

Look about you; everything you see was most likely freight carried and delivered by trucks; after all, trucks transport approximately 70% of all freight in the United States. Shippers need office equipment, furniture, consumer electronics, and clothing to be transported from one location to another.

You may discover shippers as freight brokers by researching the goods you encounter every day to learn where they are produced and how they are delivered.

7.2 Review Your Purchase History and Compare

Finding it difficult to locate shippers or feeling helpless? Examining your purchases is a good place to start. The goods you buy are produced and delivered from someplace, whether it is the receipts from the shop or your online Amazon order history.

When you're a freight broker searching for shippers, you have to be creative and think outside the box at times. Understand how businesses are linked and don't quit if one lead doesn't work out or isn't a feasible alternative; there are infinite options.

7.3 Look at the Competition

It is a normal occurrence and a driving factor of the capitalist economy that rivals any product transported by freight. Consider a big corporation such as John Deere. With manufacturing facilities in Wisconsin, Iowa, and Georgia, they proudly produce a wide range of tractors.

Even though it is a Fortune 500 business with a large market share, John Deere faces stiff competition in the tractor sector.

By selecting the industry peers option on a tool like Morningstar Financial, you may learn more about the company's rivals. Freight brokers may search any publicly listed business.

7.4 Use MacRae's Blue Book and Other Shippers Lists

MacRae's Blue Book is an industrial directory with comprehensive information on manufacturing firms. You may look for businesses depending on the goods they make, and the comprehensive information about them will even provide freight cost estimates for you to compare.

Other industrial lists, including The Industry Week 500, are excellent resources for freight brokers looking for shippers. Boeing and General Electric, for example, have a massive supply of supplies for both receiving and delivering freight. Make use of the list as a starting point for locating suppliers for these businesses.

Have you ever wondered how many components are needed to construct one of Boeing's 737 planes? There are 367,000 pieces total. Suppliers of those parts can be found all over the country (and even the world) and are frequently small to medium-sized businesses with limited resources to handle their freight.

Here's where freight brokers may use Google's magic to locate shippers.

Search for "Boeing 737 Suppliers," and you will get a comprehensive list of the aircraft's suppliers, along with business data and contact information.

7.5 Livestock, Produce, and the USDA

To meet customer demand, produce is transported across the nation. Who doesn't enjoy guacamole in the winter, especially when it is just in time for the big game? Seasonal differences in produce regions vary, but you may assume that the Midwest has corn, Texas has avocados, Florida has fruits, and the Pacific Northwest has apples. Farmers that produce crops or poultry raise cattle and other animals may be found and contacted via the USDA business listings.

7.6 Satellite View of Company Buildings

Freight brokers may utilize street views of a facility or Google Maps satellite to check whether it has shipping and receiving docks by continuing to depend on Google and being creative in their searches for shippers. You may spend hours simply walking along the streets of industrial districts, checking to see if there are any docks. Next, you may conduct some research on the business to learn more about what they do and how they transport freight.

7.7 Cold Calling Shippers

Cold calling is a viable option. After you have found a shipper, you will need to contact them to see whether they're interested in utilizing a freight broker. Sending a short email is simple, but the odds of receiving a response are slim. Calling shippers directly and being honest in your conversation is the greatest approach to connect with them.

A sales pitch isn't required and may be off-putting, but you should explain who you work for, your company's history or accomplishments, and where you're seeking to move freight to see how you can help. Remember that you are there to offer them a service, so pay attention to their requirements and how you may alleviate their problems.

You will need to figure out how the shipper presently moves freight and determine if you can do anything to take advantage of the situation. Undoubtedly, a large percentage of shippers will decline your request, but it is a numbers game, and you won't know whether you have prospective customers unless you call.

7.8 Trust, Relationships, and Load Boards

Finding shippers is only one part of the process of being a successful freight broker. When it comes to serving your shipping customers, you will need to develop connections and earn a reputation for being reliable. To accomplish so, you will need to use load boards like Truckloads, which have over 100,000 certified carriers with whom you may connect to transport freight for the shipper.

As a freight broker, you will want to cultivate relationships with carriers, particularly those who are qualified. Once you have found a carrier you can trust and with whom you have a strong working connection, stick with them and provide them the chances they want to keep the relationship going.

7.9 Get Connected

Asking other freight brokers for recommendations is one of the simplest methods to discover excellent carriers and expand your network. Joining an industry group, such as the Transportation Intermediaries Association, may help you start networking even if you don't know any other brokers (TIA). TIA is a freight broker membership organization that may help you develop connections, get access to resources, and learn about key third-party logistics issues.

Members of the TIA may search a directory for certified drivers and utilize the organization's popular TIA Watchdog function. Consider Angie's List of the trucking industry: it enables TIA members to share information on rogue operators. No-shows, unauthorized re-brokering of shipments, cancellations, theft, unjustifiable freight loss, and other problems may be reported by users.

7.10 Get What You Pay for.

You wouldn't go to a back-alley, unlicensed surgeon and ask for their best pricing if you required life-saving surgery to remove a brain tumor. If you're insured, you'd want the finest doctor money could buy. Why? Because of the greater the doctor's price, the more expertise and credentials they have. While truck driving isn't the same as brain surgery, the same principle applies: experienced drivers get paid more. Low-paying loads tend to attract low-quality drivers, whereas high-paying loads tend to attract high-quality drivers. Make sure you know the going pricing for loads comparable to yours and offer a competitive cost.

While it is possible to obtain a low-quality driver from what seems to be a high-quality carrier, many load boards contain risk-mitigation capabilities. Look for one that checks carrier credentials and offers unbiased, third-party data on carriers' operating authorization, insurance, and CSA safety ratings. You may also browse reviews of potential carriers to see what other brokers have to say about them.

7.11 Get Quality Drivers by Being a Quality Broker

Being a dependable and responsible broker is one of the greatest methods to recruit excellent carriers. That includes treating drivers the same way you want to be treated and operating your company ethically. Carriers are more inclined to perform their best job and even recommend others to you if you pay them on time, communicate politely, and follow through on your promises. If you don't treat carriers properly, though, the news will go around. Truckers speak, and you want to make sure they're talking positively about your company.

It is also crucial to grasp the trucking industry's laws and regulations, such as the Hours of Service (HOS) requirements. Maximum hourly driving restrictions, mandatory rest intervals, and sleep requirements for drivers are all established by these regulations. They are necessary to protect the safety of passengers, drivers, and other cars on the road, and drivers who break them are breaking the law. When truckers are given loads with unreasonable delivery dates, they are put in a difficult situation that jeopardizes everyone's safety on the road. Make sure your customers have reasonable expectations, and never ask a driver to remain on the road longer than the HOS rules allow.

Finally, never double-broker carriers to demonstrate that you're a trustworthy broker. Double brokering, which is not to be confused with co-brokering, occurs when a carrier (who may also operate a freight brokerage) receives cargo from a freight broker under the pretense of transporting the load but then sells it off to another carrier. Always be open and honest in your interactions. You will avoid legal wrangling and demonstrate to carriers and shippers that you're a reliable partner.

Fair brokers who pay generously and consistently recruit quality carriers. Contact Triumph Business Capital if you need help with working capital so you can pay drivers quicker (even if you're waiting for payment yourself). We can help you manage your accounts receivables and pay your carriers on your behalf.

CHAPTER 8:

The legalities and formalities

A freight broker must constantly put in efforts to maintain connections with carriers and shippers, promote your company, network with other brokers, and, of course, focus on expanding your services, in addition to the day-to-day duties. It is no surprise that achieving compliance may be difficult. Keeping up with freight broker compliance obligations, such as renewing the surety bond on schedule or the newly implemented Food Safety Rules. Failure to do so may result in the loss of time, money, and other resources. Continue reading for a summary of some of the most important compliance standards to be aware of while working as a freight broker.

8.1 Freight Broker Compliance Requirements

The Code of Federal Regulations (CFR), Part 371 - Brokers of Property, lays out the key compliance standards that every freight broker should be aware of right away. The

CFR outlines several basic criteria for brokers and a set of specific regulations for brokers dealing in-home products.

Brokers are required to maintain records of transactions, prevent Misrepresentation, not charge carriers in particular situations, and account for their income and expenditures properly. A short description of each of these criteria may be found below. A full description of these may be found in Lance Surety Bonds' freight broker compliance guide.

1. Keeping Records

Brokers must maintain comprehensive records of all transactions for three years, according to the CFR. The consignor's name and address, the bill of lading, the motor carrier's name and address, and the amount of money received by the broker in exchange for their services must all be included in these documents. These records must also be accessible to everyone who has been involved in the transaction.

2. Not Charging Carriers

Brokers may not charge carriers for services if the broker owns or has a stake in the cargo being carried. This also applies to situations when the shipper owns or is controlled by the broker, and the broker has authority over the shipment. Aside from low-cost marketing materials, brokers are not permitted to sell or give anything of value to shippers.

3. Avoiding Misrepresentation

Freight brokers have a responsibility to avoid portraying themselves as providing carrier services in any manner, according to CFR 371.7.

Any broker's advertising must mention explicitly that they provide brokerage services.

Brokers must also only execute and provide services in the name they have registered with the Federal Motor Carrier Safety Administration (FMCSA).

4. Correct Accounting

Finally, brokers must correctly account for their costs and earnings when they participate in other types of business, under 371.13. Brokerage-related revenues and costs must be differentiated and segregated from the rest of the revenues and expenses, or they must be distributed on an equitable basis when they are shared.

5. Rules for Household Goods Brokers

An entire part of the CFR is dedicated to specific regulations for home goods dealers. In summary, this section covers the following issues:

- The carriers with whom a broker may do business
- They must display the information in advertisements.

- The data they must give to shippers, as well as
- The rules for keeping written agreements with carriers in place

Because these regulations may be very complex at times, home goods dealers should study Subpart B of Part 371 of the CFR and get fully acquainted with it.

6. Food Safety Rules

The Sanitary Transportation of Human and Animal Food Guideline, published by the Food and Drug Administration (FDA) in mid-2016, is another essential rule that freight brokers must follow. For shippers and brokers with more than 500 workers or carriers with annual revenues of $27.5 million or more, the regulation went into force on April 6, 2017.

While the majority of this regulation applies to shippers and carriers, brokers are also obliged to follow it owing to the rule's wording, which includes freight brokers in its definition of "shipper" The regulation covers four major compliance areas: transportation operations, vehicles, and transportation equipment, personnel training, and record-keeping.

Brokers' responsibility in adhering to these regulations will ensure that all of their staff are well acquainted with them. Employees who deal with shippers and carriers, on the other hand, will need to ensure that these partners are following the regulations by checking or requesting that they do so. Brokers must also create clear processes and standards for ensuring such compliance, according to the FDA.

Because the Final Rule's requirements and suggestions may be complicated, the FDA has just developed a "Small Entity Compliance Guide."

7. Yearly Bond Renewal

The annual bond renewal for the freight brokers is a last but crucial compliance obligation. Maybe this may seem simple, there are often delays around certain bond renewal dates, such as October 1. This is because a significant number of brokers had to raise their bond amounts around October 1, 2013, when the FMCSA required a higher sum.

Missing the deadlines and having your license suspended by the FMCSA may result from such delays, as well as just failing to renew your bond. As a result, sureties usually send out reminders at least 60 days, often even earlier, before the renewal date.

The easiest method to avoid being caught up in delays or forgetting to renew is to renew as soon as your surety reminds you. The surety will have ample time to complete your renewal application and send your bond to the FMCSA on time if you do it this way.

CHAPTER 9:

The daily routine of the freight broker

Freight brokers serve as middlemen between shippers and carriers, arranging for freight transit. After then, the freight broker is paid a commission for their matching abilities. Truck brokers, property brokers, transportation brokers, and third-party intermediaries are used to describe freight brokers. While the freight brokering company idea is straightforward, there are many intricacies and processes to learn. The broker must know what to do, when to do it, how to do it, why it, and who to do it with.

Because this is a service-oriented company, it is only natural to get familiar with the various needs and specifications. Especially given the fast-paced atmosphere that will inevitably emerge. While genuine "on-the-job" experience is the greatest instructor, finding brokers ready to take on prospective rivals is very tough. Formal instruction from competent people assists the starting broker in putting everything into perspective and allows them to go their route. With objective instruction, the new broker gets off to a good start. Let's take a closer look at a regular day in the life of a freight broker.

After making many phone calls and contacting as many prospective shoppers as possible, the freight broker should have a database of maybe 20, 30, 40, or more shippers. The first piece of information that each broker will gather is general: what kind of cargo is being sent, where are the usual pick-up and delivery locations, what kind of vehicle is needed, are the loads LTL or full truckloads, and so on.

1. With this information in hand, the broker should begin requesting the order by calling shippers early in the morning — maybe between 7:30 and 10:30 a.m. Most shippers are putting the finishing touches on their requirements at this time. In essence, the broker is inquiring whether the shipper needs any vehicles on that specific day.

2. If the broker receives a "No," he or she moves on to the next step. The action starts when the broker strikes a "hot" one (or many) at some point.

3. After the broker has "proved" himself or herself, the shipper will contact the broker directly rather than the broker phoning the shipper. In addition, instead of searching for trucks daily, the shipper may wish to

work more proactively by looking for vehicles 3-5 days in advance.
4. The next step is to accept the shipper's order. The shipper will go through everything in detail. Any doubts the broker may have should be addressed right away. When the carriers begin phoning in, the broker must convey the proper information to them.
5. The broker will then either provide an estimate of the required rate and contact the shipper; alternatively, the broker will start asking the shipper what they want to invest. The freight broker will calculate an amount to offer the vehicle after doing certain calculations. The optimum starting point is to make a profit margin of at least 10% on each load. Profits, on the other hand, may be much higher.
6. Post these loads on online load boards as the following step. There are many load boards where loads may be placed and truck searches that can be conducted.
7. The broker will next go to their list of available trucks once these loads have been advertised. After that, the broker will contact each carrier to check if they have any trucks available. In the meantime, the broker may be getting calls from people reacting to the load boards' postings.

8. The broker is searching for a dispatcher or driver who will say, "Yes, I want the load" at some point. Sometimes the broker is unable to locate a truck. It is not like shooting fish in a barrel, but with expertise and repeat business, he will cover more and more loads and do it faster.
9. Once the broker receives the carrier's "Yes," he or she immediately contacts the shipper to inform them that the cargo is "covered."
10. The broker will then fax or email the carrier their setup material. While the carrier completes the paperwork, the broker will inspect the carrier to ensure it is properly licensed and insured. This may be done via the internet, over the phone, or through third-party sources.
11. The "confirmation" is the final item delivered to the carrier. The carrier should date and sign this document as soon as possible and return it to the broker by fax or email.
12. Once the broker gets this confirmation, he or she should contact the truck driver if the driver has not already done so. The specifics of the load and any additional instructions are subsequently provided to the driver. For example, the broker may request that the driver call when loaded, empty, or have a

problem. If the journey is longer than one day, the broker will require the driver to phone in at least once a day.

13. These are essential criteria that each broker should properly convey to the driver without exerting undue control over how the driver makes his or her delivery.

14. If a driver fails to follow general guidelines, the broker should be prepared to terminate the driver's connection. We go into a lot more depth about expectations and how to deal with drivers and trucking firms in our freight broker training.

15. Once the cargo has been delivered, and the broker has received the carrier's report, the broker will contact the shipper to inform them of the situation.

16. Any delivery issues, such as missing parts or damaged goods, should be resolved between the shipper and the carrier. The broker may interfere on occasion; but, unless the broker is irresponsible, the broker is never accountable for any missing or damaged parts.

17. Finally, the broker is ready to repeat the procedure now that the cargo has been delivered securely and on schedule.

While this practice may seem casual and uninteresting at times, this is far from the case. Most of the time, the broker will have an easy time. There will, however, be occasions when issues emerge. The broker must cope with late deliveries, carrier failure to pick up a load, damaged cargo or missing parts, and lengthy delays in picking up or delivering goods.

It is difficult to prevent issues, but it is possible to be alert and prepared to deal with them before they occur. The broker is well on his or her way to a profitable business if he or she works hard and clever for the shipper, provided the broker deals fairly with the truck and pays them on schedule.

CHAPTER 10:

Using social media to grow your freight broking business

5 Steps to Establish Your Logistics Company On Social Media

1. Post often and regularly.
2. The user's content must be relevant and attractive.
3. In the comments area, interact with your fans.
4. Sponsor the posts you make.
5. Use both images and videos to get the most out of your audience.

10.1 Why use Social Media?

As you may be aware, an increasing number of businesses are turning to social media for their public relations (PR) and marketing initiatives. But have you ever thought about why businesses utilize social media instead of more conventional marketing/advertising methods (radio, print, television, billboards), which are still effective? Here are some social media facts that will help you understand why social media has been and continues to be a successful marketing tool for businesses:

Adults between the ages of 18 and 34 are the most likely to follow a company on social media (95 percent)

71% of customers who have had a positive experience with a brand's social media service tend to suggest it to others.

Globally, there are 2.56 billion active mobile social media users, or 34% penetration; 1 million new active mobile social users are added every day.

As you can see, there is a lot of user penetration, making social media a must-have for every large or small company. On the other hand, small businesses seem to be particularly drawn to the notion of utilizing these platforms since they offer a low barrier to entry, are readily accessible, and allow advertisers to micro-target customers in ways that no other media can.

On the other hand, larger businesses (1,000+ workers) usually have an established brand that draws consumers without depending significantly on social media material. It is not that they shouldn't engage; it is just that they have more branding choices than businesses with fewer expenditures.

10.2 Facebook

Facebook is excellent for building a community of individuals who support your business and want to know where it is at all times.

This platform is ideal for sharing educational materials, driving traffic to your company's website, participating in networking groups, and posting sponsored content in the form of videos or pictures to promote your Facebook page/website.

10.3 Instagram

Surprisingly, being active on Instagram is becoming more and more of a must for logistics businesses. Companies may function with a large sample size simply because of the sheer quantity of consumers. It is also a fantastic approach to humanize your business and highlight what you're doing for the environment, the community, and your workers.

10.4 LinkedIn

One of the most cutting-edge platforms for business professionals to connect and grow their networks. This is one of the finest locations to network and interact with contact points for shipping firms, carriers, and other brokerages in the logistics industry. LinkedIn is the place to be whether you're prospecting for freight, searching for competent carriers, or looking for new opportunities.

10.5 Twitter

As you may be aware, the logistics market is similar to the stock market in that it is continuously changing owing to a variety of external factors such as weather, politics, the time of year, and so on. Twitter is a better medium than any other for staying up to speed on current events and engaging with followers. You will win if you use this application to get online conversations about your business.

Conclusion

Trucking is by far the most important mode of transportation in the United States. The trucking industry transports an astounding eighty percent of cargo in the United States. This is four times more than what is transported through rail, air, and sea. In addition, the trucking industry has given employment to approximately seven million people. Trucking revenue soared to nearly $800 billion in 2018. It is also expected to grow by 75 percent by 2026. As a result, it is one of the most rapidly expanding small business sectors in the United States. The trucking industry has had a great impact on the American economy. The economy will grind to a halt if small trucking companies stop operating. Fortunately for you, rising freight demand combined with the shortage of drivers allows you to launch your trucking company and make a lot of money. There are a few things you should know if you want to run a successful trucking company. The first step in starting a trucking company is to write a rudimentary business plan. This business plan will define your goals, determine the strategies needed to reach these goals, and galvanize you to accomplish those goals within the stipulated time. Consider your trucking business plan to be a road map to get you where you want to go. It should mention the kind of equipment you intend to use, whether you intend to buy or lease it, your financial projections, and how you intend to achieve your expansion goals.

Dispatching is one of the most crucial components of a trucking company. You can boost your trucking company's productivity and save time and money by maintaining accurate records for all of your dispatches. As an owner-operator, you will be more vulnerable to making financial errors. You could lose track of your cash flows and might fail to raise investment at the right time. You can successfully manage your cash flow by automating the trucking business invoicing system, which allows you to create, send, and track invoices and payments. When you run a trucking company, you need to keep track of your expenses and make sure your trucks are well-maintained, so they stay in good working order. The only way to ensure that your trucking business is profitable is to know how much it costs to run it. You should consider the truck maintenance and repair costs, office expenses, insurance payments, salaries, and other business expenses. Any business owner should be aware of their numbers and how their company is performing. This is because a trucking company operating in a trucking industry can easily fail due to a lack of planning and poor management. During the first five years, more than fifty percent of businesses fail. Your trucking business can succeed with the proper research, strategy, and planning.

Moreover, you should have the capability and skills to adapt to changing circumstances. In any business, having a plan and sticking to it is critical to success. When operating in the trucking industry, you should always try to deliver loads on time, maintain good relations with your dispatchers, maintain a clean driving record, and follow all federal regulations. In addition, you must pay close attention to your safety department. You must understand that successful trucking requires a lot of hard work. You should be well-versed in the various aspects of the trucking industry. You must have excellent customer service skills and be able to apply them. You won't be able to succeed unless you learn basic truck mechanics. You should try to learn how to manage your stress. While driving, you must maintain complete concentration. You must look after your health. The most important factor is that you must be enthusiastic about your business. You'll also need a dependable, efficient TMS program in addition to a sound business plan. It's because knowing where your money is going is the first step to success in business. With this system, you can keep all of your important information in one secure location that you can access at any time. This allows you to keep track of mileage, fuel consumption, invoices, dispatching, IFTA reporting, and vehicle maintenance, among other things. Profit and loss reports, as well as any other information necessary to understand your business's growth and profit potential, can be generated with just a few clicks.

<u>Thank you for reading this far! I would be extremely grateful if you would take 1 minute of your time to leave a review on Amazon about my work.</u>

Made in the USA
Coppell, TX
17 February 2022